DATE DUE			
Jul 8 '81			

THE MESSAGE OF THE BIBLE

The Message of the Bible

WILLIAM NEIL

HARPER & ROW, PUBLISHERS

SAN FRANCISCO

Cambridge London
Hagerstown Mexico City
Philadelphia São Paulo
1817 New York Sydney

THE MESSAGE OF THE BIBLE. Copyright © 1978 by A.R. Mow-
bray. All rights reserved. Printed in the United States of Amer-
ica. No part of this book may be used or reproduced in any
manner whatsoever without written permission except in the
case of brief quotations embodied in critical articles and reviews.
For information address Harper & Row, Publishers, Inc., 10
East 53rd Street, New York, NY 10022.

Designed by Pat Friday.
First Harper & Row edition published in 1980.

Library of Congress Cataloging in Publication Data

Neil, William, 1909–1979
  The message of the Bible.

  1. Bible—Criticism, interpretation, etc.
2. Bible—Theology. I. Title.
BS511.2.N39 1980   220.6'1   79–3602
ISBN 0-06-066092-9

80 81 82 83 84 10 9 8 7 6 5 4 3 2 1

Contents

Acknowledgment

The opening chapter was first published as an article in
Asking Them Questions, edited by Ronald Selby Wright
(O.U.P., 1972).

INTRODUCTION

What Meaning Does the Bible Have for Us Today?

For the best part of two thousand years the contents of the Bible have influenced the life and molded the thought of the Christian Church. For far longer than that the Jewish Church has regarded most of what is written in the Bible as its sacred Scriptures. Muslims worship the Supreme Being whose sovereignty over the created world is proclaimed there, and they venerate Abraham, Moses and Jesus. In a divided Christendom the Bible is coming more and more to be seen as the way to closer fellowship and understanding between Catholics and Protestants. No book sells more copies; no book deserves more study. Yet there is no doubt that the intelligent reading of the Bible today is hedged with difficulties.

We live in an age of science, and we are accustomed to think in terms of an evolutionary process whereby, over a period of millions of years, primitive forms of life gradually developed into more complicated organisms until eventually the animal kingdom emerged as we know it today, with man as the end product. And yet the Bible appears to claim that the whole process of creation, including all living things on land, in the sea and in the air, was completed within a week.

We often read in our newspapers of astonishing ventures into outer space, and we know that our little planet is but a speck in an apparently limitless universe, with untold galaxies stretching out to inconceivable distances, and that living creatures, of quite a different type from anything we know, may exist in other parts of this amazing world. Yet the Bible seems to know nothing of all this. Its world is this earth, and not a great deal of it, with sun, moon and stars provided largely as adjuncts, and principally for man's benefit.

We do not claim to know all that we may yet come to know about the so-called laws of nature, but at least we can say that serpents do not talk, axe-heads do not float, and men do not get carried up to the sky in fiery chariots nor do they compose psalms while they are inside a whale's belly. Yet the Bible seems to describe these and many more equally unlikely events as if they actually happened.

Clearly, then, whatever the Bible may be, it is not a reliable guide to such areas of knowledge as are dealt with by biologists, geographers, astronomers and geologists. For information on these subjects we turn to the relevant textbooks and not to the Bible. Since it was written in pre-scientific times by unscientific people, it is as unreasonable to expect it to take account of modern science as to complain that Shakespeare makes no reference in his plays to electricity or television and shows no awareness of atomic energy. We do not think any less of Shakespeare's plays because of these gaps in his knowledge. No more should it worry us that the Bible has little or nothing to say on scientific matters that is not more accurately said in modern textbooks.

Another difficulty is that although the Bible appears to be a historical account of the fortunes and misfortunes of the Jewish people, continuing into the foundation and first stage of Christianity, it is not history in our modern sense. It does not provide us with a reliable and detailed coverage of the period with which it deals. Important battles are omitted, and politically significant reigns are summarily disposed of in a few verses, while minor incidents and personages are dealt with at considerable length. What archaeologists have so far discovered in the way of evidence of the life and times of the ancient Near East confirms in general the picture that the Bible gives. But if we are looking for a factual record of the history of Israel and the early Church in the manner of Gibbon's *Decline and Fall of the Roman Empire,* or Motley's *Rise of the Dutch Republic,* we shall not find it in the Bible.

Nor should we turn to the Bible if we want to be provided with arguments for the existence of God, or speculations as to the nature of truth, the origin of evil, the possibility of immortality or the relationship between mind and matter. The kind of questions that have exercised philosophy down the ages are not the subject matter of the Bible, and we shall look in vain there for ready-made answers.

So far we have been concerned with what the Bible is not rather than with what it is. But it is important that we should not be put off reading the

Bible by looking to it for the kind of information it does not claim to provide or try to provide. It does not profess to be a guidebook to modern science, ancient history or religious philosophy. It is primarily a book of theology, a book about the knowledge of God. It is concerned, like science, with the universe, but unlike science, it is not so much concerned with how the universe works as with why there is a universe at all. It deals with history, yet not as a record of kings and battles, but as the area of human experience where God can be seen at work. Like philosophy, the Bible is occupied with the meaning and purpose of life, but it does not ask, "Is there any such meaning or purpose?" On the contrary, it starts off by assuming as self-evident a personal God who has created and sustains the universe, and in whose service all created things find their true fulfillment.

God, the world and ourselves

The Bible, then, is a book about God, the world and ourselves. It claims to answer far more fundamental questions than those that are dealt with by scientists, archaeologists or historians. It goes to the heart of the mystery that surrounds our existence and tells us why we are here, where we are going and how to get there. It deals with our life on earth in all its rich variety, its joys and sorrows, its successes and adversities, and it holds out a promise of a richer and fuller life beyond the death of our bodies. It does not claim to solve all problems or encompass all knowledge, but it claims to give us the clue to the riddle of life and to provide sign-posts pointing in the general direction we should go, but leaves us free to choose our own route to get there.

Much of what the Bible has to say to us is told in the form of stories, but the whole book itself is a story, the story of what God has done, still does, and will yet do for the world he has created and for the men and women who live in it. The Bible conveys above all the message that God cares for the world, and that because of this, at a certain point in history, he came among us in the person of Jesus Christ. From a Christian point of view, the Old Testament tells the story of the preparation for the coming of Christ, and the rest of the New Testament, after the gospels, tells of the sequel to that event.

The Old Testament differs from the New Testament in many ways. Not only is it much larger, but there is much greater variety in its contents. The main reason for this difference is that while the Old Testament is a collection of the religious writings of the Jewish nation, gathered over a period of a thousand years, the New Testament is the religious writings of a fairly small community, the Christian Church, gathered mostly during a period of no more than a century.

So while we find in the Old Testament history, poetry, proverbs, folk tales, prophetic oracles and codes of legal enactments, the New Testament consists mainly of two types of writing: gospels and letters, the gospels being fairly brief accounts of the life and teachings of Jesus, and the letters being writings to young Christian congregations by various of his followers. Yet amid all this variety, the Bible is one book; the Old and New Testaments are part of the same story.

The People of God

The thread that runs right through the Bible, and binds together the patriarchs in the book of Genesis with the young churches to whom St. Paul writes in the New Testament, is that it is all the story of the People of God. The Bible tells of the choice by God of a particular community, Israel, which was to be an example to the rest of the world of how life should be lived in harmony with God and with one another. Enlightened by God through their priests and prophets, their psalmists and wisdom scribes, they were themselves to become enlighteners of mankind, charged with the task of communicating the knowledge of God and the nature of his true service to all nations.

Because of the weakness of human nature, Israel failed in its mission. But we are meant to learn through that failure that more than human resources are needed, even with divine guidance, if the world is to become the kind of place God means it to be. So God comes into the human scene directly in the person of his Son, in the mystery of the Incarnation. Born an Israelite, of a Virgin Mother by the power of the Holy Spirit, Jesus of Nazareth begins not only a new chapter in the story of the People of God but inaugurates a new era in the history of mankind, since for the first time a man was what all men were meant to be. It was his purpose that the vocation of old Israel should be taken over by a new Israel, at first consisting of a handful of Jewish fishermen but opening its doors to Jews and Gentiles alike as the Israel of God, the Christian Church. Through the power of the Spirit that Christ gave to the Church, men and women who had committed their lives to him in obedience and service began to find their lives renewed in worship, prayer and sacrament and they went out into the world as missionaries of this good news from God, to offer to others what they themselves had received.

If we are to understand the Bible, therefore, we must begin by seeing it as a whole, as the story of one increasing purpose, as a divine plan from Genesis to Revelation. Its beginning is the intention of God to save us from ourselves, and its end is the renewal of the life of the world. Temple and Church, Jewish Law and Christian Gospel are part of the same story. Insofar as we are members of the Christian Church, we are legatees of the faith and practice of the Old Testament, bound in fellowship with Abraham, Moses and the saints of old Israel, as much as with the saints of the New Testament.

The world of the Bible and the world today

Yet there is no doubt that it requires a considerable effort of the imagination to feel that the world of the Bible, Old Testament or New Testament, is the same world as the one we live in. Perhaps it has never been more difficult than in this gadget-minded century, when television, electricity, jet planes and technological and electronic developments have revolutionized, in the West at any rate, a way of life that until recent years had gone on more or less unchanged since biblical times. The outlook and daily concerns of shepherds, farmers, villagers and fishermen are not easy to relate to life in an automated factory or a city skyscraper.

Moreover, even with the most modern translations of the Bible in our hands, we are still faced with a vocabulary and thought forms that are unfamiliar and often hard to grasp. What does the Bible mean by such words or phrases as Covenant, Kingdom of God, Messiah, justification? How do we square with modern medical and psychiatric practice the biblical assumption that disease and insanity are caused by demon possession or that the various parts of the human body—heart, liver, kidneys, bowels—are literally the sources of our emotions?

Nevertheless, whatever changes have taken place in our way of life, in our everyday vocabulary and in our scientific understanding, the Bible retains its power over men's minds because its basic concern is with things that go deeper than any of these. We want to know how to keep our feet in a world that is in disarray and confusion by finding a meaning and a purpose in all that goes on. We want to feel that life matters, that we are not like Fabre's caterpillars, crawling round and round in a dish in endless procession until they die. We have immortal longings in us, and we want to know if beauty, goodness and truth are merely words. We ask ourselves if it makes any difference what we do from day to day, or whether all will be the same a hundred years from now.

These are the big questions that men and women have always asked, and they are equally or even more relevant today. And these are the questions with which the Bible is concerned and to which it gives answers that are as valid in the twentieth century as they were when the Bible was written. The story that the Bible tells was acted out on a tiny stage in a corner of the Near East, in times far removed from our own, but the men and women who played their roles faced the same problems as we do. They shared the tensions of adolescence, middle age and declining years. They fell in love and got married, coped with the upbringing of their families, and were sometimes struck down by illness or adversity, sometimes exhilarated with success.

Stumbling, falling, picking themselves up, saints and sinners, wise and foolish, rich and poor, strong and weak—this is human nature as we know it today, and this is how it has always been. But the men and women of the Bible saw life in a context that made sense. They were able to confront whatever befell them because they believed in God, believed that they mattered, believed that God had a purpose for them. They saw themselves as members of a community whose mission was reconciliation; the breaking down of barriers of class, race and color, which separated men from men; and the breaking down of political and economic barriers, which separated society from God.

And so to learn the secret of coping with life, with adversity, suffering and death, and to learn how we can help to make our society healthier and happier for all concerned, we turn to the Bible. As we have seen, it claims that this is the intention of God, Creator of the universe and Lord of history, and it outlines his plan for achieving this purpose. The working out of this plan, and the realization of this purpose, depend upon the existence of a community, the People of God, consisting of men and women who have been called by God and who have responded to his summons. They, in their turn, have become this kind of community, dedicated to the service of God, because of certain things that have happened in history.

Poetry, myth and legend

It is for this reason that the Bible is not a collection of moral precepts, or a handbook to what constitutes the good life, but a record of the events that brought this community, the Christian Church, into being. Here, however, another difficulty arises. For when we turn to the Bible expecting to find such a factual narrative, we discover that the Bible is never content to record facts without at the same time drawing attention to their significance. What we are given consistently is fact plus interpretation. When, for example, at the beginning of the story of Israel's fortunes, Abraham leaves Mesopotamia and begins the long trek which eventually brings him to Canaan, a secular historian would describe this journey as a normal tribal migration, common among the nomadic people in that part of the world. The Bible, however, sees Abraham's departure from his homeland as a direct response to a summons from God.

But apart from being more interested in the meaning of events than in prosaic descriptions of the events themselves, omitting those that they consider to have no particular significance in the story of the People of God, and underlining those that have, the biblical writers use poetry, myth and legend where they think these will serve their purpose better than factual statements. The Creation story in the first chapter of Genesis, for example, is not an attempt to give a scientific account of the origin of the universe and its inhabitants. It is a splendid poem, celebrating the sovereign power of God, who brought into being all that exists, and affirming right at the beginning of the Bible that the created world is not the result of a series of flukes or accidents, or the product of some blind fate, but the work of a purposeful and beneficent Creator.

Most of us would recognize that the power of evil in the world is a hard fact with which we have to reckon. However we explain it, it is more than the sum total of the lapses of ordinary fallible mortals. Manifestations of mob violence in race riots, or the calculated sadism of Nazi concentration camps and gas chambers, have a demonic character, as have their instigators and organizers. The Bible establishes this fact of experience in the myth of the fallen angels, which by its very obscurity suggests, more vividly than any lengthy sociological study, the demonic quality of human depravity and perversion.

The most memorable event in the Old Testament is the escape of the Israelites, under the leadership of Moses, from the threat of extinction in Pharaoh's slave gangs. It marked the beginning of Israel's life as a nation and her distinctive faith and moral code. But in reading the record of the Exodus, we have to sift the probable historical happenings from the mass of legends that have grown up around it and are included in the narrative. Yet these very legends convey, better than the sober pen of a historian, Israel's profound conviction that this was an act of God whereby he dramatically called his people out of darkness into light, out of a living death into the gateway to freedom. So it is with the legends that are told of later figures such as Elijah and Elisha. They do not provide us with material for factual biographies, but like the legends told of the early Christian saints, they reflect the deep impression these men made on their contemporaries and tell us much about the kind of people they were.

Is the Old Testament reliable?

But the question obviously arises, if the Bible deals in interpretation more than in fact, in theology more than in history, and if its writers were equally ready to use poetry, myths and legends in telling their story, how much of it can we believe? Let us deal with the Old and New Testaments separately, for the answer is different in each case. The earliest narrative writing in the Old Testament probably dates from the tenth century B.C. in the reign of Solomon. It contains stories of the patriarchs dating back to the time of Abraham, about seven centuries earlier. Such stories were in all likelihood preserved at various sanctuaries and handed on by word of mouth to successive generations.

Although archaeologists tell us that the general picture given in the Bible of these early times corresponds to what excavations reveal of the habits and customs of the ancient Near East, we cannot regard the stories of the patriarchs as historical in the modern sense. There is no reason to doubt that Abraham, Isaac and Jacob were historical figures or that their distinctive differences in personal character have been faithfully preserved. Oriental memories were better trained than our own. Moreover, in an age where there were fewer distractions, and men depended on storytellers and ballad singers rather than on the written word, there was a check on the details of a story exercised by the community, which would object, like a small child today who is being told a fairy story, if the narrator departed from the familiar form of the tale.

But when all is said and done, it would be too much to expect that conversations could be handed on accurately for centuries, that incidents in the life of one patriarch could not be mistakenly attributed to another, and that pious tales would not tend to grow in the telling. As we have seen, legends grew up around the Exodus, and if we compare the books of Joshua and Judges, we can see for ourselves that the idealized picture given in Joshua of a whirlwind conquest of Canaan by the Israelites is not borne out by the more sober narrative of Judges. We are on more solid ground when we come to the so-called historical books of Samuel and Kings. But even here we should remember that the Hebrews included these books among the "Former Prophets," and regarded them principally as illustrative material showing that the teaching of the "Latter Prophets"—Amos, Hosea, Isaiah and the rest—had been proven to be correct by the actual course of events in Israel's history.

As far as the Old Testament is concerned, modern scholarship would generally agree that the early chapters of Genesis, the first eleven chapters, are not history at all but myths or parables. From chapter twelve to the end of the book of Genesis (Abraham to Joseph), there is more legend than history, while from the Exodus onward there is more history than legend. Each incident or passage has to be examined and weighed critically on its own merits, with the aid of the commentaries that are now available in such plenty.

By and large, however, the broad sweep of the story that the Old Testament tells is vouched for not only by the independent evidence of the great prophets, who lived through much of it and who provide a running commentary on the events of their times, but also by what has so far been discovered by archaeologists in Mesopotamia, Egypt and Palestine itself. It should also be added that our obsession, born of our upbringing in an age of science, with the question, "Did this or that happen precisely as it is described in the Bible?" was not shared by the ancient Hebrews. They were much more concerned to ask, "What is the point of this story? What is it saying to us?" It would therefore not occur to them to ask whether in fact Jonah was swallowed by a whale or whether Lot's wife was actually turned into a pillar of salt. In those cases they would look for the lesson that the story was trying to teach.

Is the New Testament reliable?

When we turn to the New Testament, both the problem and the answer are very different. It is much more important that we should know where we stand with regard to the life and teaching of Jesus and the growth of the early Church than that we should know whether Moses had a magic rod or if Elijah was fed by ravens. Unless we can be reasonably certain that what is recorded in the gospels and in the book of Acts did in fact happen more or less as it is described and is not a mixture of myths and legends, then the Christian faith is built upon sand and the creeds of the Church are meaningless.

We must, however, be sensible about this. There was no miraculous preservation of the New Testament, guarding it from all possible error, any more than in the case of the Old Testament. We cannot say with absolute certainty, "These are exactly the words that Jesus spoke on such and such an occasion" or, "This is precisely what happened at such and such a place at such and such a time." On the face of it we should say that a short, crisp saying of Jesus, such as those contained in the Sermon on the Mount, probably often repeated and carefully memorized by his disciples, is more likely to be accurately preserved than the recollection of a single event, perhaps startling, like the story of the Transfiguration.

We must make allowance for the fallibility of human memories, for occasional misunderstanding, for pious exaggeration. Above all we must remember that in the New Testament, as in the Old, it is the meaning of the events rather than the bare record of what happened that interests the writers most. The authors of the gospels did not set out to write biographies of Jesus, otherwise they would have said much more about his appearance, his boyhood and young manhood, and his work as a carpenter in Nazareth. St. Luke, in writing in the book of Acts of the story of the early Church, would have needed far more than twenty-eight short chapters if he had intended to tell the whole story of these thirty momentous years. The New Testament writers had to select, omit, amend and interpret the material that came into their hands.

Once the gospels were written, they were subject to the same vicissitudes as other ancient writings. Copying manuscripts by hand for circulation gave rise to errors caused by scribes leaving out words or lines, repeating words, and so on. From time to time some scribe would correct what he thought was a mistake, or add some comment of his own. By painstaking scholarship over the past century, most of these intentional or unintentional errors have been detected and put right, but a margin of doubt always remains.

Despite these qualifications, however, which must be made if we are dealing responsibly with the New Testament, we have every reason to say that we have in the gospels and in the book of Acts all that we need to know about the life and teaching of Jesus and the earliest stage of the Church that he founded. What we find there is not the product of inventive Christian mythmakers but reliable evidence that we can trace back to people who actually saw and heard what is now recorded in permanent form.

The divine drama

If we turn to the question of how best to read the Bible, there is no single answer. Much depends on the individual. Some prefer to follow a course of daily Bible readings with the help of a commentary, or notes in pamphlet form provided by one of the Bible-reading societies. Others will make use of a lectionary. Others, again, will find it best to read through a book at a sitting. Fewer, perhaps, will undertake to begin at Genesis and work through to Revelation. There is no golden rule in this matter.

But whatever method we adopt, it is essential that we should have at the back of our minds—or preferably in the forefront—a picture of the Bible as a whole, otherwise the particular passage we are reading may be as meaningless as an isolated piece of a jigsaw puzzle. We may think of the whole Bible as a great tapestry, like the Bayeux Tapestry, which tells the story of the acts of God in history. Perhaps even better, since the figures on tapestries can often appear formal and wooden, we may think of it as a historical pageant, with living characters and plenty of action. Best of all would be to think of the Bible as a great drama, with God in the title role and a cast that includes patriarchs and kings, prophets and apostles, but also a large number of ordinary men and women. However, we are not merely spectators of the drama, for we are included in the cast, and the play still goes on.

Try to look at the Bible as this great drama of the acts of God, and think of the first few chapters of Genesis as a prologue to the drama, the picture of men and women as God meant them to be and the picture of us as we are. It is a contemporary picture, because we are all Adam and Eve, and Cain and Abel. We are all the men who try to build the Tower of Babel and make ourselves gods. The prologue is our human situation. Then comes Act I, the rest of the Old Testament. It is the story of how God chose a people to be the means of bringing mankind to its senses and making the world the kind of place it ought to be. It is a long act, because we have to learn through the experience of other men and women, these characters in the Old Testament, the mistakes we make, and the follies we are guilty of. They have been guilty of them too, and from them we can learn. But above all we have to be shown by their failure that we need more than good advice from prophets and psalmists to bring us to God.

So the drama moves on to Act II in the pages of the gospels. God comes himself into the human scene, comes down to our level to lift us up to his, to give us the power of new life through the Holy Spirit. The rest of the New Testament, Act III, is the sequel. It is the story of how the gospel worked out in practice. Beginning with a handful of men and women, this reformed community of the People of God went out into the world, following the example of Christ, committed to him and empowered by his Spirit. They went out to turn the world upside down, to reconcile man with man, race with race, and class with class. And Act III still goes on wherever men and women in the name of Christ are trying to carry on Christ's work.

But so often this is difficult, and so often we lose heart. That is why the Bible does not leave us wondering how it will all end. It gives us an epilogue in the book of Revelation, which shows us in marvelous imagery and poetry the ultimate end of the purpose of God: the gathering of all his people in his presence. Since the outcome is in God's hands and not in ours, the final message of the divine drama is to put our trust in him and in his Word, which he has given us for our comfort and our inspiration.

BOOK 1

The Body of the Old Testament

I

The Old Testament View of God and Man

God

The most significant feature of the idea of God in the Old Testament appears in one of the most frequently used descriptions of him: I am Yahweh your God who brought you out of the land of Egypt. In other words, the Old Testament sees God not as an abstract principle, an object of speculation, but as an active force affecting men's lives and the course of events—as indeed a "living God." Hebrew religion is poles apart from philosophic contemplation of the Absolute; it is concrete and practical. God is known primarily by what he does. The Old Testament has therefore no interest in generalizations about the metaphysical nature of God. All its interest is bent upon men's experience of God in their own lives and in the life of the nation. What the original religious beliefs of the Hebrews might have been nobody knows for certain. The meaning of their names for God—Elohim, El Shaddai, El Elyon—must be largely conjectured. What is clear, however, is that from the Exodus onward, Yahweh and Israel were inextricably bound together in a unique partnership. They were Yahweh's people, and Yahweh was their god.

It is important to remember the different approach to the question of God in our own and in ancient times in the East. The attitude of skeptical philosophic enquiry that is part of the legacy of Greece to our modern world was completely foreign to the Oriental mind. Our method, borrowed from Greece, is to amass all the facts of nature and experience and then argue that therefore there must be such a being as God to account for them. We should admit the right of a man on intellectual grounds to be an atheist, an agnostic, a materialist. We might doubt whether his conclusions met the facts of experience, whether they were a reasonable interpretation of the sum total of our own observation and that of past generations, but we should understand the basis on which the atheist's or materialist's point of view was constructed. But such a point of view as atheism, materialism, or even agnosticism was unknown to the ancient Oriental mind. Every tribe had its god whether it was Hittite, Canaanite or Israelite; later every nation had its god or collection of gods. Religion was as much a part of people's lives as their food and clothing. They never doubted the existence of supernatural beings any more than they doubted the solidity of the ground they trod on. So we look in vain in the Old Testament for any proofs of the being of God. The Hebrews needed no proof of Yahweh's existence; they took him for granted. Even in the so-called philosophical literature of the Old Testament, such as Job and Ecclesiastes, no matter how deep Job's despair or how radical Ecclesiastes' skepticism, they never question the fact phasis from the outward attributes of personality—such as speech, hearing—and sight—to the inner qualities of the spirit. The Old Testament at its highest is unashamedly anthropomorphic—so, let us not forget, was Christ himself. To admit that is simply to admit that unless we talk of God in anthropomorphic language, we cannot talk of him at all. We can only use the language of our ordinary human experience, and provided we remember that no human thought or language can possibly be adequate to comprehend or describe the Power behind the universe, when we talk of God's "personality" we are ascribing to him the highest value that we know. The God of Israel at its religious best is a God who cannot be represented by any image or idol, who is further above man than man is above the meanest creature of the earth, but who nevertheless loves and pities, inspires and strengthens mankind, who is higher than the heavens but yet responds to men of humble and contrite heart.

From trickery to transcendent morality

In one of the old patriarchal stories (Gen. 12: 10–20) Abraham, to save his skin, passes off his wife as his sister. Pharaoh takes Sarah into his harem, whereupon Yahweh promptly afflicts Egypt with plagues until Pharaoh realizes his error. It is a far cry from the kind of God who encourages a deception of this kind to the God of Amos and Isaiah. Yet it is true to say that while the Hebrew idea of the character of God shows steady growth and development, the relationship between Yahweh and his people was a moral one from the very beginning. It was as Wheeler Robinson says in *The Religious Ideas of the Old Testament,* p. 66, "like a friendship between two men, beginning in some act of generous help rendered by the stronger to the weaker, behind which act the larger heart and mind are gradually discerned." As their own moral standards grew, so did their conception of the character of God. The peak achievement in this respect was, of course, the work of the eighth-century prophets, such as Amos and Hosea, but even before then a pronounced and healthy moral tone is very evident. It is a high tribute, for example, to the state of public morality in 1000 B.C. in Israel when the prophet Nathan can denounce his sovereign to his face for his adultery with Bathsheba and get away with it. It is safe to say that in no other Oriental country of the time could that have happened. Similarly, when Elijah stands up to Ahab it is because God condemns the theft of a poor man's vineyard as much as the encroachment of Jezebel's Tyrian religion. The various legal documents—the Ten Commandments, the Book of the Covenant— show clearly that before the days of the great prophets, the kind of conduct God demanded was not merely ritualistic, but was concerned with such things as the care of widows and orphans, and generosity to debtors and slaves. Obviously the kind of God who demanded these things was conceived of as having a very pronounced moral character himself. With the classical prophets this becomes explicit. Amos, with his insistence on the justice of God and the unique moral responsibility of Israel because of its unique privileges, and his condemnation of the vices of his times, sets the tone for the rest. Hosea implements this with his emphasis on the love of God, and in these two conceptions, righteousness and mercy, all the other attributes are comprehended. Isaiah crowns them with his strong sense of God's holiness, that is, his otherness, his transcendence, and we are left with the picture that became fundamental for later Israel, the legacy of the prophets, of "the majesty of a righteous and loving Person."

Why the world and man?

There is progress too in the developing picture of Yahweh as Lord of nature. He is never identified with the land like the Canaanite baals; it is rather that his scope extends from that of the god who brings thunderstorms to help the Israelites in a tight corner to the Creator of the universe as depicted in Job 28 or Proverbs 8. But when all is said and done, the Old Testament looks on the created world in all its majestic splendor and marvelous infinity as chiefly a battleground for the moral issues of human life. The crown of creation is man—Ps. 8— made a little lower than the angels and given all created things to be subject to him. It is through man that Yahweh achieves his purpose, molding him as the potter molds the clay (Jer. 18:6). That purpose is that men should learn to say, "I delight to do thy will O my God" (Ps. 40:8)—in other words, the fellowship of men with God consisting of moral obedience is the aim to which the whole scheme of things is directed. Thus the heart of Old Testament religion is that it brings God and man face to face in a moral relationship—in the willing service of man to his Creator. That God's purpose will ultimately be achieved, the Old Testament has no shadow of doubt.

Man

No less than in their ideas about God did the Hebrews find that they had to develop their ideas about man. The process is not so obvious because the Old Testament is primarily concerned with God, not with man; it is theocentric, not anthropocentric. There was no parallel to the Greek interest in the virtues for their own sake but only as they were involved in obedience to Yahweh. Hence primitive ideas about man survived longer than primitive ideas about God. Where the eighth-century prophets challenged worn out conceptions of the nature of God, they left undisturbed the popular conceptions of the nature of man. What happened was a gradual transformation of outlook as time went on rather than any marked change as a result of striking contributions by individual thinkers. The most significant and far-reaching advance ever made in the field of religion was when Israel harnessed morality to religious faith. That seems so obvious a step to us today that we perhaps fail to appreciate the importance of it. It was in fact not obvious to any nation but the Hebrews, which is what constitutes the uniqueness of their contribution to humanity. It was they who with all their primitive ideas about God and man grasped the root of the matter that the true worship of God was the service of clean hands and a pure heart. Having perceived that truth, all that remained was to follow out its implications. In so doing, what had been an obscure Oriental cult like dozens of others became transformed into a universal religion. Let us see now the effect that the working out of these implications had on the Old Testament view of human personality.

Hebrew psychology

The material that the prophets had to work on in their transformation of the Old Testament ideas about man was more or less the same psychology as is common to all primitive peoples—the idea of a breath-soul (and blood-soul), the attribution of psychical functions to physical organs, and the belief that any kind of unusual behavior or experience was due to possession by alien spirits. The Hebrews started from the common observation that when a man died his breath stopped: therefore his breath must be his life, his soul, the center of his being (*Nephesh*). When Elijah brought back to life the widow of Zarephath's son (I Kings 17:22), the boy's "soul" returned to him, clearly meaning his breath, the thing that gave him life. From the idea that the breath-soul was the animating principle, it came to denote all inward consciousness—emotions, thoughts, desires. The second feature of biblical psychology is that various parts of the body are credited with different conscious functions—heart, liver, kidneys, bowels, hands and so on. When the Psalmist says his heart and flesh cry out (84:2), he means it literally; so does the author of Proverbs when he says his kidneys shall rejoice (23:6). "My heart is not haughty nor my eyes lofty" (Ps. 131:1). "The ear trieth words as the palate tasteth meat" (Job 34:3). These are not poetic fancies or figures of speech but statements of believed facts. It is not difficult to see the origin of this in such things as a sinking feeling in the pit of the stomach, cold shivers down the spine and so on. What happened was, however, that the heart predominated and came to have as important a significance as the breath-soul; it became equated with consciousness. The tendency was to attribute intellectual activity to the heart and emotional activity to the soul. So that "to love the Lord thy God with all thy heart and with all thy soul and with all thy might" (Deut. 6:5) means to love God with your whole personality. The third feature is the use of the word "spirit," *ruach.* This word originally meant "wind" and continued to mean "wind," but in addition it was used for that universal belief of ancient times in possession by supernatural spirits, whether good or bad. These spirits that blew into a man like wind into a canyon could either make him mad like Saul (I Sam. 18:10) or strong like Samson (Jud. 15:14); they might be the work of demons or the work of Yahweh. As time went on it came to be regarded as the normal endowment of normal people—their "spirit"—in the same way as their "soul." Yet they were never quite equated. Spirit always retained its original connotation as something connected with the supernatural. It was always with a man's spirit, not with his soul, that he sought contact with God. It is the door by which God's spirit enters, the common factor in worship. God is spirit and man is flesh, yet it is as Isaiah says "with my spirit within me that I seek longingly for thee" (26:9). We should equate the word today perhaps with subconsciousness, through which our conscious thoughts and aspirations find access to, and are enriched by, hidden sources of power and the fountainhead of all goodness, beauty and truth. The result of this psychological outlook of the Old Testament is that in practice there is no distinction made between body and soul. Human nature is one—a compound of soul, heart and spirit. The body is not something apart from the mind or spirit; it is a complex physical organism animated by a breath-soul. Take away the breath-soul, the principle of life, and nothing remains. Hence the idea of the immortality of the soul is ruled out. The dead go to Sheol where they live not as conscious souls or spirits but as shadows without form or personality. This, then, was the foundation on which the prophets had to build their conception of man's place in the universe.

Man and his Maker

The prophets more or less accepted the psychology outlined above. What happened, however, was that their progressive insight into the nature of God affected their views of the status and destiny of man. This influence is seen by contrasting once again the two Creation narratives. In the first, God makes man of a mixture of clay and breathes life into his nostrils (Gen. 2:7). Here man is a creature like any other animal—body suffused by breath-soul and no more—and there is no suggestion of spirit. In the second, the operative idea is that man is made in the image of God (Gen. 1:27). Whatever that may mean, it implies a clear separation of man from other creatures and a unique relationship with God. So this relationship becomes increasingly in the Old Testament the theme of poet and prophet. Continually they stress man's dependence on God for everything he has and is (Ps. 139). A new status is given to mankind as a result: his moral consciousness acquires enhanced value as the reflection of the will of God. Characteristic too is the growing prominence of the Spirit of God as a source of strength and power. God's call upon men for service was too high a standard for mortal creatures; only by inbreathing of God's own spirit could a man hope to fulfill God's demands. So Ezekiel talks of God imparting a new spirit to the people, taking away their hearts of stone and giving them hearts of flesh (11:19 f.). Just as the many gods became one God, the only true God, so the many demonic spirits have become one Spirit, the only true Spirit. So the Psalmist prays, "Take not thy Holy Spirit *ruach* from me" (51:11), and Joel awaits an outpouring of the Spirit upon all flesh (2:28). It is the Spirit of God working upon the human spirit that alone has power to change evil to good and to make the impossible possible.

Corporate personality

One of the important differences between the Hebrews and ourselves lies in their emphasis on what is best called "corporate personality." The unit right up to the Exile was not the individual but the community. It might be the family, the tribe, or it might be the nation, but the individual derived what significance he had from membership in it, not from any self-existent status. Hence the unfailing stress on "the people," the personification of Israel. What mattered in the early days was not that a man should be right with Yahweh but that people should be. Consequently, what appear to be some of the most bloodthirsty incidents in the Old Testament were not only regarded as normal, but even held to be demanded by Yahweh. A man who committed a crime did not stand alone; he involved his whole family or his tribe. If it was a crime against another tribe, they demanded satisfaction not only from himself but even from his descendants. If it was a crime against Yahweh, the only expiation was that the man's family should suffer with him. In neither case was there any vindictiveness; it was the justice of the times, no more than the social conscience that today would insist on imprisonment for housebreaking. Thus David (2 Sam. 21) finds by oracular means that the reason for a famine is that Saul had slaughtered most of the tribe of Gideon. The survivors are asked to name the penalty; they ask for the lives of seven of Saul's descendants. When these men—to our minds completely guiltless—have been killed and their bodies hung in the wind before Yahweh, his wrath is appeased, and the famine stops. So with Achan (Josh. 7), who stole some of the spoil of Jericho that had been earmarked for Yahweh. He had aroused Yahweh's displeasure against the whole nation, and they suffered defeat as a result; therefore, Achan must suffer, yet not only Achan but his family and cattle as well. So as a matter of course the accusers of Daniel who are cast into the lions' den are accompanied by their wives and children (Dan. 6:24). These, then, are not examples of spite but the normal implications of corporate personality, expressed clearly in the Second Commandment where God is said to punish the crimes of the father up to the third and fourth generation after him. Although Israel was tending more and more to make the individual alone responsible for misdeeds and to look on the individual rather than the nation as the unit, it was not until Jeremiah's idea of the New Covenant that God would make with each individual that it became explicit (31:33–4). Partly, no doubt, this was due to the collapse of the nation, partly to the failure of Josiah's reforms on a national basis, partly to Jeremiah's own intense personal relationship to Yahweh. Ezekiel confirmed this (18:4) with his doctrine that the soul that sinned alone would suffer. Nevertheless, though the individual came into his own in a way, the sense of corporate personality, social solidarity and national unity was never lost. In the highest conception of the national role and vocation in the Old Testament —the Servant of II Isaiah—the unit is the community, the individual's justification is his place in that society.

Future life

The strong sense of corporate personality meant among other things that the Hebrew gave little thought to any future life. He lived on in his chil-

dren in a much deeper sense than we should use the
same expression today. The most glowing prospect
that could be held out to a man was that his progeny
would grow as thick as grass (Job 5:25). When a
man died, that was to all intents and purposes the
end of him. Some dim shadow of his former self
lived on in Sheol, "the land of darkness and of the
shadow of death" (Job 10:21). Samuel, on emerg-
ing from it (I Sam. 28:6 ff.) at the call of the witch
of Endor, was recognizable, but Sheol seems to
have lain outside the proper domain of Yahweh. It
may have been a survival idea from the days of
ancestor worship, or a growth of the idea of a family grave, but it was a prospect that roused no en-
thusiasm, that of a colorless, insubstantial, amoral
existence (Job 3:17–19; Is. 14:9–11). Two tenden-
cies contributed to change this: one, the collapse of
the hope of national survival after the Exile, and
two, the extension of the sovereignty of Yahweh to
include Sheol as well, for example, Ps. 139:8: "If
I make my bed in Sheol behold thou art there."
Ezekiel's doctrine of individual retribution in this
life being contradicted by all the facts, men sought
some deeper explanation of the injustices of life.
We have seen such tentative gropings after a solution in Job (14:13–15; 19:25–7) and in Ps. 73.
There, however, and in other cases it is not so much
an established doctrine as individual ventures of
faith. At its best the Old Testament would suggest
that the man who has established a personal relationship to God has something that neither mis-
chance nor even death can interrupt. Parallel with
this, however, grew a cruder form of belief in bod-

ily resurrection as we have seen in the apocalyptic literature, for example, Is. 26:19 and Dan. 12:2. The basis for bodily resurrection was, of course, the Hebrew idea of the inseparability of body and soul, and in both cases it is not a universal resurrection of the dead, but is confined to the faithful of Israel in the first case and the martyrs and villains of the writer's times in the second. Both of them think of the future life as being lived within the impending Messianic kingdom that will be established on the earth. These higher and lower views of a future life (if we may call them so), that of Ps. 73 and that of Dan. 12:2, which the Old Testament does little more than suggest, were both carried over into the New Testament times, the one ultimately by St. Paul and the other by the Pharisees.

The Legacy of the Prophets

Let us now try to summarize the contribution of the great Old Testament prophets to religious thought and assess its importance and value. In the early stages of their history, the aspect of God that presented itself most vividly to the Hebrews, as indeed to all primitive peoples, was that strange, uncanny quality that has been called "the Numinous." Holiness was the characteristic of God that was most stressed, but it was holiness in the sense of otherness and untouchability. It was bound up with ritual and taboos that were designed to protect the worshiper from the effects of contact with God, or with things or persons sacred to him. As time went on religion became more and more a matter of doing the proper things at the proper times: keeping the festivals, fulfilling the ceremonial, offering the sacrifices. The service of God was something that had no bearing on life outside the sanctuary, and however impressive it was—and with its massive temples, its pageantry and liturgy, its processions and music, it must have been very impressive indeed—the religion of Israel was rapidly heading for that divorce between religion and morality that so many other religions have experienced when the worship of their god is in one compartment and ethical principles in another (e.g., Greece and India).

It was at this point that Amos made his protest at Bethel. His message, which had the effect of a thunderbolt, was that the whole paraphernalia of ritual and ceremonial was so much waste of time. It had nothing to do with God. What God wanted was moral service, not the slaughter of animals and incantations. Amos was as conscious of the holiness of God as any priest of the Temple, but, he said, it is not by a careful observance of taboos and correct formulas that God's wrath can be averted and his favor gained, but by the kind of life you live. This note, common to all the prophets, is the *first* of their great achievements. It is best summarized by these words from the book of Micah (6:8): "He has showed you, O man, what is good, and what does the Lord require of you but to do justice, and to love kindness, and to walk humbly with your God . . . ?" *Morality then must go hand in hand with religion*—which of course means that religion becomes subject to reason. So long as the service of God was a frantic attempt by ritual, prayer and sacrifice to keep on the right side of an incalculable Being whose chief characteristic was that you never knew what he was going to do next, it was bound to be completely beyond rational understanding. The Numinous would become more Numinous, holiness would become more irrational, greater and greater attention would be lavished on observance of the taboos and formalities, and the whole business would bear less and less relation to ordinary life. But whenever this sense of the Numinous is interpreted in ethical terms, whenever holiness takes on a moral quality, then religion comes within the field of rational comprehension. That does not mean, of course, that mystery is ruled out, that religion then becomes as demonstrable as a mathematical problem. But it means that the religious emotions, instead of being expended on irrational and meaningless formalities, are directed into the channels of ethical behavior.

The prophets' message is in short that a religious man's duty is not to lavish his devotion on an elaborate cultus, but to be kind and honest and truthful and charitable. To us this message may be a commonplace. To the Hebrews it was by no means so. True, when the prophets spoke, they spoke always as those who were not teaching something new, but recalling men to old truth. We have seen how they were the champions of the nomadic ideal and how the tension between the standards of the desert and the temptations of civilization runs right through Hebrew history. But in the desert a comparatively high ethic went hand in hand with an extremely primitive religion. Yahweh-worship in Moses' day was more irrational than when Amos took his stand at Bethel. It is the great achievement of the prophets that they harmonize these two sides of religious life by pointing out that unless the worshipers are those who do what is right, or at least try to, their worship is a mockery. Holiness is not an amoral, irrational quality, but is to be equated with righteousness. Instead of cringing in terror before the uncanny, people must stand in awe before the morally perfect. It is thus through their conception of the true service of Yahweh as being right behavior that the prophets are led to make their *second* great contribution, in providing *a new insight into the nature of God.*

Notice how this insight came about. It was not by abstract philosophic discussion among scholars on the nature and properties of the deity. It was a direct consequence of a sharpening of men's conscience. Religion is often rightly condemned by moralists for lagging behind in ethical standards. The Greek gods behaved in a way that no decent Greek of Plato's day—let alone a moralist—would have countenanced. And in more modern times there is the classic admission by the orthodox fire-and brimstone-preacher that the Almighty is compelled to do many things in his official capacity that he would scorn to do in his private capacity. When men feel that the character of their god is less admirable than the highest ethical thought of their times, then there is something wrong in their ideas about their god. Sometimes, however, when the deity is conceived as an extremely remote, other-worldly being like the Chinese Shang-Ti, it is impossible to apply any standards to it at all. Confucius found this and so turned his back on the official religion as having no future and concentrated on moral teaching. Yahweh, on the other hand, was not conceived of by the early Hebrews as an abstract principle, but as a very lively, active warrior leader, albeit a crude and incalculable one. But while such a god of fire and slaughter, capricious and moody, might do well enough for the desert,

he would hardly do for the civilized life of Canaan.
That is why the prophets up to the eighth century
—Elijah, Elisha and the others—strike us as semi-
barbaric figures. They do not speak our language.
They are trying to bring not only the ethical standards of the desert into civilized life—that aspect
finds our ready response—but also the Yahweh of
the desert as well and, as C. H. Dodd says, Yahweh
of Sinai amid the settled life of Canaan "has something of the uncouth look of a fighting squire from
an older time, scorning the softness of courtiers and
the wiliness of prosperous hucksters, yet a little
awkward and self-conscious" in the presence of the
more cultured deities of the city. The god of the
ninth-century prophets is still the irritable, petulant, cruel—if rather splendid—god of the desert.
It was due to Amos and his successors that this
rather wild and incalculable god of Israel was seen
to be a rational, moral being, not only adapted to
civilization in Canaan but to civilization anywhere.
They saw clearly that God could not be any less
moral than they believed he wanted men to be. If
God demanded honesty, kindness, integrity and
truthfulness from men, he must be at least as kind
and upright and honest himself.

In their estimate of the character of God, the
prophets emphasize three aspects: his consistency,
his justice and his mercy.

God's consistency

The one thing that Yahweh was not in the days
before the eighth century was *consistent*. He was

incalculable. On the one hand, he was the kind of god who could issue the Ten Commandments to Moses; on the other hand, he could be guilty of the most astonishing and contradictory behavior. Cain and Abel do their best to please him with their different types of offering. For no reason at all he accepts one and rejects the other (Gen. 4:4–5). Moses is singled out while a fugitive in Midian to be Yahweh's leader of Israel out of Egypt and sets off in high spirits, but on the way back Yahweh, again for no reason, tries to kill him (Ex. 4:24). Elijah has to take him to task for causing the death of his landlady's son, and after entreaties coupled with black magic, Yahweh changes his mind, and the boy returns to life (I Kings 17:20–22).

This sort of thing, the great prophets say, is a complete misrepresentation of Yahweh's character. He is above all consistent and never capricious. We may not always understand why things happen, but we can be assured that they are not the result of some whim of a glorified tribal chieftain. God is absolute, but he cannot be false to himself. If a thing pleases him today, it will please him tomorrow also; if he disapproves, his disapproval is on principle and not a passing fancy. He is not a man that he should repent; he will not be turned from his purpose by any number of burnt offerings; he must be true to himself. To realize the tremendous step forward that religion took at this point, it is worth noting the difference between this conception of the prophets and that of Mohammed more than a thousand years later. Mohammed in the Koran is so anxious to preserve the idea of the omnipotence of God that he turns him into a benevolent sultan whose decisions are arbitrary, who can be judged by no standards or principles except that of his own unique power. This assumption of the prophets that God is subject to law lies at the heart of all their teaching and leads them to insist on his justice.

God's justice

The prophets saw that if God is consistent in his actions, if he is subject to self-imposed laws, then his attitude toward men, whether friendly or hostile, must have good reasons behind it. Like all their predecessors, the prophets were satisfied that whatever misfortune or disaster a nation suffered was due to some offence against the deity. Their forebears, however, like all primitive people, were content to regard such misfortunes or disasters as the result of some offense that they had unwittingly committed or some breach of the taboo. Yahweh's wrath was something that they could never be sure of avoiding, hence the multiplication of ritual observances as an insurance against it. The prophets, on the other hand, have seen that a good man is not subject to outbursts of petulant rage, visiting his wrath on the first person he sees; therefore, neither can God's wrath be irrational. Hence their insistence on the principle of retributive justice. If Yahweh is angry—and his anger is shown by such phenomena as an earthquake, cloudburst, drought, famine and the like—it is not without cause. It is because the people have sinned against his laws, not by inadvertently breaking a taboo or omitting a prescribed ritual, but by their dishonesty, their oppression, their loose living. It is this conviction of the inherent justice of things that leads all of them to attribute the decline in the nation's fortunes to the national crime sheet and to foretell greater disaster still. War, destruction and banishment will surely overtake the Jews, and it will be nothing more than they have deserved. It is a logic that is irresistible and in a broad sense unquestionably true. The great empires of the past that have fallen in ruin have done so generally because of inward corruption and a betrayal of the ideals that guided them in their rise to power. A civilization that obeys the moral laws prospers, while one in which greed and bribery, self-interest, luxury and cruelty predominate is doomed to extinction. But the principle is not so clear when it is applied to individuals. We have seen Ezekiel's statement of it: that a man's misfortunes are due to his own sins. The prophets on the whole were not concerned so much with individuals as with the nation. They look on Israel as a whole, and so far their diagnosis is sound. Later thinkers, as we shall see, more concerned with individuals than nations, find that the prophets have not tackled the problem at its deepest level, and the writer of Job and the Psalmist have to think through the problem again. It becomes in the end the big question mark of the Old Testament. Why does a good man suffer? The Old Testament can give no answer because life for the prophets ends in the grave. It is only when religious thought rises to life after death that any answer can be given.

Meantime, however, the prophets' conclusion is nonetheless momentous, that at the very heart of things a principle of justice lies embedded.

God's mercy

Yet it does not seem as if the prophets were finally content that an exact retribution of evil for evil was all that there was to be said. They were, after all, not logicians but men of feeling and imagination. They were not slaves of cast-iron principles; they saw that life was greater than logic, that room must be made in human thinking for what appear to be contradictions, and that when an idea is pushed so far that it ceases to be true to life it must be modified. So Hosea, for example, as convinced as Amos was of the stern principle of divine justice, nevertheless felt the tug at his own heartstrings for the wife who had betrayed and deserted him and who on all counts of justice should have been banished forever. But he found he still loved her and he asked himself can Yahweh feel any less toward Israel? There must be something more in God's nature than stern relentless justice. And so he adds to the conception of the justice of God the mercy of God, that can forgive even the impenitent, and receive back the hardened offender, and blot out the past misdeeds. Just because God is so much above mortal men, just because his holiness is so great, so therefore his power of forgiving love must be infinitely greater than man's. This belief crops up again in Jeremiah's idea of the New Covenant written on men's hearts, and in Ezekiel's thought that God will take away the hearts of stone and replace them with hearts of flesh. The prophets on the whole would have said that in order that God should have mercy, it was necessary for men first to repent. But they would not—especially II Isaiah—deny that even before man's repentance come the mercy and love of God. They feel somehow that it is because it is God's nature that he shows mercy, not because men have done anything to deserve it (see Is. 55:6–9). Here again the prophets leave an unsolved problem: How can God's mercy and God's justice be reconciled? This too remains unanswered until New Testament times. But in their estimate of the nature of God, the prophets unerringly grasped and stated the truth that the otherness of God, his holiness, his Numinous quality, his difference from men, lay not in his being able to indulge in capricious whims or irrational tantrums, but in being more just, more loving and more self-consistent than mere mortal men could ever hope to be.

The *third* contribution of the prophets to the development of religious ideas lies in their *enlargement of the scope of God's activity.* The old Hebrew belief had been in the local gods of their own wells, or hills, or trees. Then Yahweh, whose domain was Sinai, became mobile insofar as he visited Israel in Egypt and traveled in the Ark to Canaan. On arrival there he had to dispute the lordship of the land with the local baals whose claims were well established. When he finally won the contest over Melkart of Tyre, he was the god of Israel and all the land

pertaining thereto, but no one felt that he had any
concern with lands and peoples that lay beyond. It
was again left to the eighth-century prophets to
break new ground. It was not altogether new
ground when we remember that the old Creation
myths, which existed before the time of the prophets, attributed worldwide functions to the god of
Israel, and the legends of the crossing of the Red
Sea and the plagues of Egypt had not confined Yahweh to territory strictly his own. But his existence
was so closely bound up with Israel that whatever
he did was thought of as being for their special
benefit—even including the creation of the world.
Amos and his successors would have none of this:

> *What are you more than Ethiopians*
> *O Israelites? Yahweh asks;*
> *I brought you up from Egypt? Yes.*
>   *And Philistines from Crete*
>   *From Kir the Aramaeans.*
>   *(Amos 9:7)*

Yahweh is the molder of world history, not merely
the history of the Hebrews. Israel looked forward
to a great Day of Yahweh, when the great nations
who plagued them and served other gods would be
destroyed and Israel would become supreme. The
prophets say, "Yes: that Day will come but it will
not be a day of vindication for Israel, but a day of
vindication of God's righteousness, and Israel will
suffer with the rest—only more so because of the
special privileges and opportunities she has had."
So the prophets can see in Assyria and Babylon, in
the hated Gentile oppressors, instruments in God's

hand to serve his ends of punishing evil wherever it is found, even among his chosen folk. (How remarkable a step forward this idea was can be realized when we consider that nations today have not yet overcome the tendency invariably to identify their cause in war with righteousness and invoke God's blessing as a matter of course without respect to the rights or wrongs of the case.)

Yahweh, then, is the lord of history according to the prophets, and all his actions subserve the one purpose of establishing the reign of righteousness on the earth. Yet there is an important limitation. The prophets do not simply think of all humanity as one homogeneous family. In their thoughts Israel remains the main channel through which God works. Even Jeremiah, in his conception of individual response to God, sees the regenerated individual as part of the community of Israel; and Isaiah of Babylon, the most advanced in his idea of the role of Israel as the servant of God to enlighten mankind, still has room in his thought for the supremacy of Israel over all other nations. It was a difficult business to avoid the temptation to make Israel the special favorite of God, and the prophets did not finally solve the tension between Yahweh the universal God, the only God, the Lord of all nations, and Yahweh the God of the Chosen People. This conflict too remained unsolved until New Testament times, and indeed in the intervening years, the tendency was rather to favor the narrower nationalistic view, perhaps of necessity.

The *fourth* point at which the prophets make their impact upon religious thought is the insight they give us into *personal religion.* When we read of Moses and the burning bush, we feel sure that behind it lies some deep religious experience that we can only guess at; so when Elijah on Sinai hears after the noise of the storm and the earthquake the voice of God speaking to him in the silence, we recognize again something that is genuine and real behind the outside shell of the narrative. But here in the classical prophets are men whom we can mostly understand, who are dealing with a type of life and civilization that is more or less familiar, and who reveal to us in their speaking and writing the inmost experiences of their own spiritual life. We can see behind the psychic phenomena, the strange symbolism, the bizarre visions, men in touch with a world beyond the one they lived in, communing with sources of power and inspiration beyond themselves. They are obviously neither the victims of self-deception nor the victims of the automatic mechanical experiences of the modern medium. The results of their experience are neither a chaotic jumble of haphazard fancies nor prosaic prognostications of future events, but are new and powerful ethical and religious principles that have commended themselves to all generations since their day as insight of the highest and most spiritual order. What the prophets say is something that they themselves have first deeply felt. They feel that they are men with a mission, to speak the truth as they see it in defiance of all opposition without fear or favor. Their own lives, their own experience, are living witnesses of the reality of the ideas they utter. We see in them, in their doubts and fears, their hopes and faith, the deepest expression of things we can authenticate in our own experience. We can dimly share Isaiah's sense of the majesty of God, Hosea's conviction of his tenderness and Jeremiah's trust amid perplexity and despair. It is not the least of the merits of the prophets that they unlock the door of personal faith to the storm-tossed world of the human spirit.

So, then, to sum up, the prophets were not social or political reformers concerned with the structure of society for its own sake, but men who out of their own personal relationship to God spoke a message to their times in harmony with the insight that came to them in the silence of their communion with him. They are revolutionaries, but they are God's revolutionaries. Again we must emphasize that they are not philosophers brooding on the problems of the world in the tranquillity of the study, but men in the midst of the mêlée themselves fighting and suffering, sharing the problems and disappointments and defeats. It is that very fact that gives timelessness to their message, much more than if they had tried to enunciate general principles in an abstract setting. Their message, because it is spoken in concrete terms, burns with a conviction that is red hot with urgency. It has that same quality as had the poets and painters who have been most notably localized and time conditioned. Raphael's Madonnas are no less eternally beautiful because he dressed them like Italian peasants. Burns is not less but more of a universal lyrical genius because his daisies are Scottish daisies in an Ayrshire field and his banks and braes are those of his own bonnie Doon.

Because the prophets were men of their age, time conditioned and human, we shall not expect to find them infallible. Not only were they proven wrong in some of their judgments of facts, but some of their ideas of God and his ways were imperfect and wrong. That men are inspired does not mean that they are free of the limitations from which every man and every age suffers, limitations of knowledge and of apprehension. Humanity learns but slowly of the mysteries that lie beyond its ken, and many aspects of divine truth have still to be revealed. But when we assess the contribution of the great prophets of the Old Testament to the religious thought and experience of the world, it can only deepen our consciousness that in the realm of the knowledge of God, in which we ourselves nearly three thousand years later are the merest learners, they were supreme masters.

III

The Legacy of History

The Bible is an account of how a certain otherwise insignificant nation reached certain highly significant religious convictions. But it is not a scholastic production that smells of the lamp, as if the writers had abstracted themselves from common society and developed their thoughts without reference to the ordinary life of men. On the contrary, the religion of the Bible is religion through life—through the vicissitudes of political history, the rise and fall of empires, the economic changes of an expanding nation, the personal fortunes and misfortunes of national leaders and everyday men and women. The motif that runs right through the Bible is that if God is to be found anywhere, he is to be found in the hurly-burly of life, working through history, through the good and evil of social organisms. The setting of the religious ideas of the Bible is, then, a historical setting. Our material for building such a history is partly the biblical narratives and partly the historical records of the surrounding nations (mostly discovered through archaeological studies). How far the book of Genesis is fact and how far fiction is a question that no one can answer.

Obviously the first eleven chapters are not historical in our sense of the word. They are teaching theology in the form of stories that read like fairy tales but are full of profound religious truth. There is no agreement among scholars as to how much historical value attaches to the stories of the patriarchs—Abraham and his successors—as affording data for the early chapters of Israel's history. All are agreed, however, that we cannot take these stories at their face value.

The general picture of the Israelites in the days of the patriarchs is one of peaceful shepherds, mostly on the move, sometimes on one side, and sometimes on the other side of Jordan, ranging from the north of Palestine to the borders of Egypt. The end of the patriarchal age sees them in fact migrating into Egyptian territory. The familiar Joseph story tells how this precocious youth was sold by his envious brothers into slavery in Egypt and by a combination of piety and good fortune won favor with the Pharaoh and became his prime minister, thus being in a position to offer a home there to his father and brothers in a time of famine. There is no real reason why the substance of this story should not be true. Famine outside with the promise of corn in Egypt would be sufficient attraction for some of the tribes to make a prolonged stay in the lands to the east of the Goshen delta. The story seems to fit into Egyptian history because about this time—1700–1550 B.C.—the Semitic Hyksos kings had gained the upper hand in Egypt and would not be averse to some of their fellow Semites entering the country. When the Hyksos kings were expelled, to say that "there arose a new king over Egypt who knew not Joseph" (Ex. 1:8) was probably putting it mildly, and the words may well cover the changeover from a pro-Israelite dynasty to a strongly hostile one. At all events when we next see the Israelites, they are providing slave labor for the Egyptians—probably recruited by raids on their pasturelands and not involving the whole people. The next development was the greatest episode in Israel's ancient history—indeed, perhaps in all their history—which has left its mark on every branch of their literature and life: their escape from thralldom in Egypt under the leadership of Moses, known ever after as the Exodus.

Moses

Here, all the historians are agreed, we are at last on solid ground. The leadership of a great personality and a sensational deliverance from Egypt are so strongly embedded in national tradition that they must have a basis in history. The fact of the Exodus is celebrated to this day by the Jews throughout the world in their Passover services every year. It runs like the motif of a symphony right through their subsequent history. It has therefore been said that if we do not accept the Moses of the Old Testament as a historical person, we should have to invent someone to take his place. For it cannot be denied that there was a dominating personality in existence at this critical point in Israel's history—a personality as significant in fact as in the later unification of the Arab tribes by Mohammed. Moreover, no proud nation would ever invent such a story as its own enslavement to a foreign power any more than any religion would invent a story that its founder had suffered the ignominy of death on a cross if these things had not in fact happened. So that beneath the highly colored narrative of the Exodus around which has grown the customary accretion of legend lies an indisputable historic fact of a deliverance of the Hebrews from bondage in Egypt, accompanied by some memorable events and under the leadership of a national hero. If as seems to be the case not all the tribes were thus enslaved, it is clear that those who were became afterward the dominating element in the subsequent history of the people and imprinted on it the marks of their experience. So, then, the Exodus may be summarized thus: At the beginning of the thirteenth century B.C., under the leadership of Moses, those members of the Israelite tribes who had been in slavery in Egypt escaped from it in circumstances that convinced them that Yahweh was behind their escape and that an unusual combination of natural happenings prepared their minds for a new kind of relationship to one another and to Yahweh, the god who had delivered them.

The Covenant

For all this is merely the prelude to what constitutes the birth of the nation and the real genius of Moses. He was not merely the revolutionary leader who rallied around him the oppressed labor gangs and led them out to freedom; he was the statesman who made Israel a people. His task was to weld the tribes together—tribes that differed in their religious as much as in their political attachments and that were so strongly individualistic that for centuries afterward each tended to plough its own furrow. The tribal sense was a permanent feature of the Hebrew makeup. Only with the rise of the monarchy did unification become a reality and then not for long.

We have no means of finding out how many Israelites came out of Egypt. Adding the figures of fighting men given in Num. 1:20–47 to women and children might indicate about two million people. Even in these present days of mass migrations on the Continent, the problem of feeding and moving such a host would be a nightmare. In Moses' time it would have been an impossibility. We may take it that the actual number of fugitives to begin with was small—representatives of various clans who had been forced into slave labor as individuals —but that as they journeyed out of Egypt, they gathered strength as they went. A movement of this kind would tend to start with a small nucleus of picked men around whom larger numbers would gather. So that what started as a limited company— perhaps 5000—became in time a mass migration.

The basis on which Moses amalgamated the tribes was religion. There was no other basis in those days that would have sufficed. Everything points to the fact that until then each tribe of the Hebrews had its own god, and tribal life revolved around religious ritual and taboos. Moses' task was to unite them around a new god who could now obviously be none other than Yahweh, the one who had revealed himself to Moses in the burning bush and who had brought them safely out of Egypt. Put in more prosaic language, Yahweh was in all likelihood the local god of the sacred mountain in Midian where Moses had lived as a fugitive from Egyptian justice. While there, he had a religious experience, which is interpreted in the Bible in the primitive symbol of the burning bush; that for him is the turning point in his life. He goes back to Egypt convinced that he is Yahweh's man and Yahweh is his god, and with that conviction and the added proof of the apparently miraculous deliverance from Egypt, he has the religious basis for the unification of the clans. Whatever the origin of the Hebrew word for Yahweh—and nobody knows— he was clearly the kind of god the tribes needed at that moment: a mountain god, a storm god, a fire god and a warrior god. Living in the desert himself, Yahweh would know the needs of wandering clansmen—their quest for water and pasture.

And so a bargain is struck—a covenant is made —that Yahweh shall be their god and they shall be his people. With primitive ritual the union is accomplished (Ex. 24:3–8). An altar is created at the foot of the sacred mountain symbolizing Yahweh, and the people stand in front. Animals are killed and half the blood is sprinkled on the altar and the other half on the people. Thus the people and Yahweh become symbolically one—he adopts them and they adopt him. What was the text of this Covenant between Yahweh and Israel? Verse 24:7 mentions that the Book of the Covenant was read by

Moses before the symbolic union takes place. At one time this text was thought to be the laws contained in chapters 21–23, but these are mostly laws designed for an agricultural community, not for a nomadic age. Further they can be paralleled in Hammurabi's and other codes of the Middle East. These chapters are much more probably the Hebrew version of part of the common heritage of laws and customs in that part of the world. The Covenant was surely something deeper and more significant than that material, and the view of most scholars now is that it was the Decalogue of Ex. 20:1–17 in possibly a slightly shorter form. The Ten Commandments, then, are the terms of the Covenant. Yahweh will keep his bargain and protect the tribes; they in return will be his people and keep these laws. Whatever be the limitations of a code of prohibitions like the Decalogue, it nevertheless singles out Moses as not only a statesman but the first great creative religious thinker in Israel. Much in the story of Moses is uncertain, but the important facts about him are beyond dispute: he found Israel a race of serfs and disorganized clans, and he left them free and united under their new god Yahweh, with a code that is still one of the great achievements of moral insight anywhere.

The Exile

In this short sketch of Israel's history, we may confine ourselves to the two main events in their long and checkered story covering seven hundred years between the Exodus and the Exile. Having been delivered from probable annihilation in Egypt, the tribes made their way to Canaan, their Promised Land, where they established a kingdom under three remarkable rulers: Saul, David and Solomon. The last of the three, Solomon, despite his legendary reputation for wisdom, sowed the seeds of disintegration by his lack of statecraft. After his death, the nation divided into two puppet states, Israel and Judah, and was led by a series of mostly incompetent rulers who proved no match for the great warlords of Assyria and Babylon as they ravaged the small countries of the Middle East. Israel ceased to exist as a nation in 722 B.C., victim of Assyrian ruthlessness, and nearly a century and a half later, in 587, Judah and its capital city Jerusalem fell to Nebuchadnezzar and his Babylonian hordes. The conquered Hebrews were carried off in chains across the desert to Babylon.

Exile and return

The best authority for the last stages of the kingdom of Judah is the book of Jeremiah. He lived through Josiah's Reformation, through the first attack on Jerusalem and deportation to Babylon in 598, and through the siege and fall of the city in 587. His role was that of Cassandra, and it was not a popular one, but despite various threats and attempts on his life, he saw the whole sad story through. Eventually he was compelled to flee to Egypt with other notables after the murder of Gedaliah, the regent appointed by Babylon. There they seem to have joined one of the various Jewish colonies that had sprung up in that country, and no

more is heard of them. Jeremiah's prophecies shed
light on the times he lived in, and his biography,
which is combined with his prophecies to form the
book of Jeremiah, is written by a man who is alive
to the big events that are taking place around him.
Once Jerusalem has fallen and interest shifts to the
exiled Hebrews in Babylon, the best guide is the
prophet Ezekiel. He was one of those who had
been deported in the first batch in 598, and from
him we get many useful pointers to the conditions
under which the exiled people lived. The Exile
lasted fifty years and made an indelible impression
on the Jewish mind. It ranks with the Exodus as one
of the great events that molded their national life
and thought. In the religious sphere, which is after
all the only sphere that really matters in ancient
Jewish history, it was all important. Now there is no
longer a Hebrew kingdom so that politically the
nation has ceased to exist. It is not even a vassal of
an empire, but in the eyes of anyone but a Hebrew
an insignificant racial group without status and
without a future. Historically speaking that view
was true; in a deeper sense, no view could have
been more inaccurate.

The Jews in Babylon 587–538

It is often thought that the Exile involved the
whole nation. This is not the case. According to
Jeremiah 52, the total deportation amounted to
4600. This number presumably represents men
only; adding women and children, the number
might be approximately 15,000. The accounts
given in II Kings 24 and 25 suggest that almost the

whole nation was evacuated, but this does not correspond with subsequent events. The exiles in Babylon seem to have lived in tolerable comfort. Chapter 29 of the book of Jeremiah consists of a letter that he sent to the first batch of deportees, and from it they seem to have had freedom to build their own houses, plant gardens and intermarry. He advises them to look forward to a seventy-year stay. In fact, he was twenty years out. They seem to have lived in various settlements and to have been allowed to earn their own livelihood. With true Hebrew acumen, they appear to have made the most of their opportunities and to have amassed considerable fortunes from trade. They were allowed to live together according to their old communities and to practice their own religion. There was always, however, the hope that something would happen to destroy the power of Babylon and thereby reverse their fortunes. Everything pointed to big events impending. Babylon had four new kings and two revolutions in six years. The exiles had enough historical sense to know what that meant. Israel's downfall had come in the same way. In 538 the empire of Babylon fell, overthrown by the new power of Persia and its ruler Cyrus. The excitement of the exiles while these events were impending can be gauged from the writings of II Isaiah (i.e., Is. 40–55). They are told to take heart, God is using Cyrus as a rod to break the back of Babylon. The dawn is at hand. Even if the indications of ill treatment (42:22 and 51:23) were not by this time universal, there was the inborn longing of freedom-loving people for release. A year after Cyrus conquered Babylon, an edict was issued allowing them to return to Jerusalem.

The Jews in Palestine 587–538

The position of those Jews who were left in Palestine was less fortunate. After the murder of Gedaliah, another governor would no doubt be appointed to keep order for Babylon and taxation would not be light. In addition, their old enemies seem to have rejoiced in an opportunity to wipe off old scores now that they had the chance. Ezekiel indulges in some hearty cursing of these jackals and prophesies Yahweh's revenge. Although Mizpah had been at first the center of the new government, it seems that Jerusalem was not so completely destroyed and soon became the center of the community. The homes of the wealthy and the public buildings were presumably the only ones to suffer. The temple had been partly destroyed, but it was an easy matter to erect an altar. Yet although for some the temple became again the center of worship, for many all the old abuses and some new ones were back again. Ishtar worship and Sun worship brought their attendant immorality. In any case, no one living in a land that has just been a battlefield can have a particularly cheerful outlook. The main note is despondency, as in Lamentations 1 and 3, changing to hope as the news comes of the fall of Babylon (Is. 21:1-2).

The return of the Exiles 537

Cyrus seems to have been one of the most enlightened rulers the world has ever seen. Instead of oppressing his new dominions—which consisted of the Babylonian Empire plus his own and was therefore the greatest empire there had ever been—he tried to placate them. He encouraged them in their own religious practices and, if they were exiles, sent them back home. Naturally the Jews shared in this policy. Some returned to Jerusalem in 537 under Sheshbazzar and found the temple walls still standing, though in a dilapidated state. As we have seen, new cults had been introduced, but Yahweh was still worshiped. The inhabitants of Palestine had become used to the mixture and the exiles joined them. The wealthiest Jews had remained in Babylon; those who came back were too busy earning a living to worry about building the temple. There was a period of seventeen years when nothing happened. Then in 520, when Darius was king of Persia, a second batch of exiles returned, including the prophets Haggai and Zechariah. Under their inspiration the reconditioning of the temple was taken in hand and finished in four years. The Zerubbabel and Joshua mentioned in the book of Ezra seem to have been the leaders of this second expedition. From then until 444 there is a gap in the records. Some light is shed, however, on this period by III Isaiah (Is. 56–66) and Malachi who are reckoned to have been living in Palestine during this time. They give a picture of a peaceful land, at first living up to the standards that Zechariah had set but deteriorating as time goes on. Religion tends to become formal; those who have made money since returning are indifferent to the hardships of the poor; injustice is rife. There is a great lack of leadership and, apart from a small section that still kept their standards high, the general tone is bad. In 444 the leader appeared.

Nehemiah

Nehemiah was of an exiled Jerusalem family. He had made good and had become cupbearer to King Artaxerxes. While the court was at Susa during the winter of 445–44, he heard of the plight of his countrymen in Jerusalem. It appeared that they had started to rebuild the city but that the hostile Samaritans had appealed to King Artaxerxes to make them stop. The king agreed, and armed with his authority, they had forced the builders to down tools. Nehemiah's sympathies were aroused; he broached the subject to the king when the wine was on the table (Neh. 2:1), asking permission to return to Jerusalem to organize the repair of the city wall. The king—who seems to have been unreliable in other things—reversed his previous decision and gave Nehemiah permission and authority to call on the imperial officials in the neighborhood to help him, making him in effect governor of Jerusalem. When Nehemiah reached Palestine he found he had two kinds of opposition to contend with. Not only were the Samaritans hostile, but also many of the Jerusalem Jews were as well. To understand this hostility, we must remember that the characteristic mark of the attitude of the Jews in exile was bound to be conservatism and exclusiveness. Suddenly transported into a foreign land, they had to insist in self-defense upon their Jewishness;

all the traditions, both cultural and religious, which were familiar to Israel were doubly emphasized. Nehemiah shared this point of view. It seemed appalling to him and the other exiles that Jerusalem the holy city should not be fenced off and safeguarded from foreign influences, especially the insidious influence of their former kinsmen of the Northern Kingdom.

Most of the Jews in Jerusalem, however, including the priesthood, took a more liberal view. They were not averse to foreign influence; they particularly felt strong affinities to the Samaritans who traditionally worshiped the same God, were Israelites like themselves and were prepared to be friendly. It was under pressure from the few exclusive Jews in Jerusalem who shared Nehemiah's outlook that the rebuilding of the city walls had started. On his arrival at Jerusalem, Nehemiah found himself at one with the exclusive section and at variance with the majority. At first he did not mention his project and inspected the damage by night (Neh. 2:12–18). Nehemiah was a man of strong personality. His rebuilding of the wall was only a means to an end—namely, the reestablishment of the Chosen People as a rigidly particularistic religious group, having no contact with the outside world. However much we are attracted by the more liberal attitude of the Palestinian Jews, it was the uncompromising orthodoxy of the Babylonian exiles transferred back through Nehemiah and later through Ezra that made the New Testament possible. The alternative would have been disintegration and submersion. All that was characteristic of the Hebrew background would have been dissolved in the hodgepodge of religious and moral practice of surrounding nations.

Opposition to the new governor, then, came from two sources. Sanballat, governor of Samaria, was not able to do much openly as Nehemiah had the king's authority. He could, however, encourage disaffection within the town itself. But in spite of all opposition, the wall was built. Chapter 4 of Nehemiah gives a vivid picture of Nehemiah's methods and precautions. Having completed his task, he redistributed the wealth of the community, set about populating Jerusalem from the country districts and then returned to court. On a second visit to Jerusalem, he appears more as a religious reformer, and all his reforms are directed toward enforcing the same specifically Jewish observances. The exclusiveness of Nehemiah was carried a stage further by Ezra.

Ezra

Ezra was a priest who came to Jerusalem from Babylon in 397, filled with a holy zeal to restore the worship of the Palestinian Jews to what he considered to be its proper and original purity—which really meant to bring it into line with the practices of the ultra-orthodox in Babylon. They had obviously not indulged in mixed marriages there, therefore neither should the returned exiles. So Ezra thunders against intermarriage with non-Jews, or people with mixed blood, and seems to have been successful. Those already married had to get rid of

their wives—a regulation of which the Aryan Law
of Hitler was an inverted replica. Ezra's other
achievement was the promulgation of the (Old Testament) Law. What that was precisely no one
knows. It clearly meant bringing the Palestinian
Jews into line with the Jews of the Exile and most
likely consisted of those parts of the Pentateuch
that emphasize racial purity and exclusiveness, circumcision, sabbath observance and holy days.
However necessary the work of Ezra was for the
preservation of the Jewish tradition intact during
the next few centuries until the Christian era, our
sympathies go much more wholeheartedly to two
other writers. First is the author of the little book
of Ruth, which dates from Ezra's time. This book
though purporting to tell a charming little idyll
innocently enough, produces a large-sized sting in
the tail by pointing out that the great King David
was himself the great-grandson of Ruth, who was
a foreigner. And second is the writer of the book
of Jonah, whose hero resembles Ezra and is told by
Yahweh that the world was not made for Jews
alone.

Persian Period 538–330

While world events took their course under
Cyrus, Cambyses, Darius, Xerxes, Artaxerxes and
their successors on the Persian imperial throne, the
scattered remnants of the Hebrew kingdoms lived
in a political backwater. They played no part on the
world stage. They became more and more self-
centered and self-conscious. While in exile in Baby-

lon, as we have seen, the temple and all that it had meant, and should mean again, focused the interests of their ablest men. Its ritual came to have almost supernatural significance. Instead of being the mere husk of worship, it became a complicated rigmarole that had to be meticulously adhered to. On return to Palestine, this obsession with the temple rites was put into practice. Jerusalem became a theocracy—a community governed on a religious basis and centered round the temple, where the priests were responsible for the government of not only ecclesiastical but civil affairs as well. It was they who were responsible for the ever-increasing prominence that the Law came to have in Jewish life. Every detail of the daily round was regulated by clear-cut injunctions based on obedience to God.

The book of Leviticus that comes from this period gives a clear idea of how the Hebrew mind was then shaping. On their return to Palestine, the Jews were confined to a small section of territory twenty or thirty miles square around Jerusalem. On east, west and south, their old enemies had established their claims; on the north, their only chance of mixing with their old kinsmen, the Samaritans, was prohibited by Ezra. While they were of too little importance to be dragged into world affairs as a nation, they were not too small to be affected by the hardships of a subject people. They were liable to pay tribute and provide men for the Persian army, and having no army of their own, they were subject to any depredations of marauding bands. So we leave the Hebrews now on the eve of the rise to power of Alexander the Great, having sketched the period that affects the Old Testament. The next age, the Greek period, is that of the Apocrypha; the next again, the Roman, is the age of the New Testament.

Summary

We have now followed the fortunes of the Hebrews up to the end of the Old Testament period. We have seen the nation rising from the impact of desert tribes upon a settled agricultural population and how this desert warrior strain, though far below the settled community of Palestine in cultural attainments, nevertheless obtained the leadership and molded the history of the first independent kingdom there. That this rise was made possible by the concern of the ruling world powers with other matters at the time—or by their temporary weakness—is admitted, but the qualities of Israelite leadership also cannot be denied. We have seen how, despite the succession of great personalities in their history who always recalled them to a sense of their own unique traditions, the country invariably slipped back in the intervening periods into ineffective drifting with the prevailing currents, and how eventually, by being false to their own best standards, they came to grief, lost their kingdom and became a tiny racial group clinging to a few acres of mountain soil.

Politically, then, their achievements in the long run were negligible. Yet their legacy is incomparably greater than that of any of the great empires that overwhelmed them. Through all their vicissitudes, the one thing that never left them was their consciousness of being a peculiar people—of standing in a unique relationship to their god Yahweh. Whether they prospered or perished depended on their obedience to him.

We have noted earlier that the Bible is not a book of history but a book of religion in a historical setting—a book that tells how a nation formed its beliefs out of the things that happened. The ancient Hebrews did not make their mark on the world by their contributions to statecraft and imperial politics. What size their kingdom was or whether it ceased to be is a matter of little moment. Their legacy was their religion.

The Message of Job

The book of Job is the greatest masterpiece in the Old Testament. It is not only a literary triumph but the full flowering of Hebrew wisdom. It is religious philosophy in the form of a superb dramatic poem. Its problem is the moral order of the universe: Why does a good man suffer? The answer it gives is the highest, except Isaiah (I 52:13–53:12) that can be given short of the New Testament. In a sense it confesses the bankruptcy of the Wisdom school— the answer to this, the greatest riddle of the universe, cannot be supplied by taking thought. But the greatness of the book does not lie so much in the positive answers that it gives to a problem that is even to this day a mystery but in the intense human interest of the character of Job and the inspiring spectacle of a man's victory over the chances and changes of life.

The book is the imaginative work of a religious dramatist of genius who, like Shakespeare, takes an old story from folklore or popular history and weaves it into the stuff of tragedy. It appears that Job was a traditional figure well known in Israel, most likely renowned for his patient endurance of trials and vindicated by being restored to fortune. The motif is common enough in religious folktales. This skeleton is taken by the unknown author of the book as we have it and built up into a dramatic unity. The date is probably somewhere in the fifth century B.C. The book is carefully and symmetrically constructed. It opens with a prologue and closes with an epilogue, both in prose. The main body of the work consists of three cycles of dialogue in poetry. There are one or two obviously later interpolations that interrupt the rhythmic flow of the argument. They should be taken out of the text and read separately; namely, the magnificent poem on Wisdom (chap. 28), the redundant speech of the pious Elihu (chaps. 32–37) and perhaps the poems about the hippopotamus and the crocodile (40:15–41:34). (Notice also that in chapter 27 before verse 7, the words "then answered Zophar the Naamathite and said" should be introduced, i.e., the whole chapter is not a speech by Job, only down to verse 6. The introductory sentence to Zophar's speech has to be supplied.)

We have already glanced at the problem that the author of Job faced up to in its historical setting. It was a problem that became more acute as time went on. When Yahweh was a capricious, irrational, Oriental potentate, what happened to mere mortals was all in the luck of the game. The eighth-century prophets had, however, made it clear that God is not irrational but rational, just and merciful. Obedience to him is rewarded, and disobedience is punished. But as the Jews had no belief in any afterlife, apart from Sheol where there was no conscious existence, the rewards and punishments must be apportioned in this life or not at all. This answer satisfied as long as the nation was the unit; sooner or later, by and large, the nation paid for its misdeeds and prospered for its virtues. But when the nation ceased to exist as a nation and the individual within society became the new unit, a new answer had to be found. Jeremiah and Ezekiel both stressed the responsibility of the individual for his conduct, especially Ezekiel who insisted that each man suffered or prospered on his own merits alone. This rather facile solution was accepted as a popular working faith by the authors of the Proverbs. Ecclesiastes, however, was not satisfied. He saw that it was not true, but he had no answer to give apart from the suggestion that as there was little apparent reason for anything that happened, the best thing to do was to grin and bear it. The writer of Job is a much deeper and more spiritual thinker than Ecclesiastes. He is a man who cannot toss the problem aside as a matter of the luck of the draw; he wants to find some reason behind the things that happen. And if he cannot find an adequate reason, he will at least not be content to leave his hero with some rather materialistic and superficial philosophy of life like Ecclesiastes. Let us see, then, what he makes of it.

Prologue (chapters 1–2)

We are given a picture of the patriarch Job himself—a native of Uz, not a Jew—who was a model of excellence of character, "perfect and upright, one that feared God and eschewed evil." Corresponding to the popular belief, he was therefore blessed with a lavish abundance of this world's goods, "the greatest man in all the east." Heaven smiled upon him for his piety. Later references in the book suggest that this piety was no stilted formalism. He was "the father of the oppressed and of those who had none to help them." When he sat as a judge in the marketplace, "righteousness clothed him" there, and his justice was "a robe and diadem." He "broke the jaws of the wicked and plucked the spoil out of his teeth," and humble in the midst of his power, he "did not despise the cause of his manservant or his maidservant when they contended with him," knowing that "He who had made him had made them" and that "One Hand had fashioned them both in the womb." Above all he was the friend of the poor, "the blessing of him that was ready to perish came upon him" and he "made the widow's heart to sing for joy."

If, then, such an upright, honest, lovable man, who did more than his duty to God and his neighbor, came to any grief or suffered any affliction, the orthodox doctrine of do well and prosper, do evil and pay, was woefully false. And this is precisely what had happened according to the popular folktale. But the folktale gave no explanation except an ultimate restitution of his worldly goods and greater prosperity than before. One poet is not content with this explanation, and he draws the veil aside from the secret council of heaven. There we find Yahweh enthroned among his angels, one of whom, called the Adversary, or Satan, comes in as he says, "From going to and fro in the earth and from walking up and down in it." His function seems to be that of a malicious sprite rather than anything else. When Yahweh proudly reminds him of his most faithful servant Job, the wily spirit suggests that Job's piety is not without reason. He is so blessed with worldly prosperity that there is no reason why he should be other than virtuous. And so Yahweh agrees to put Job to the test. Satan is to have power to shake the alleged props of Job's piety: his goods and chattels, his sons and daughters, everything but his own skin may be harmed and despoiled.

So the scene is set for the drama that is to follow, and our position in it is that of the spectator in the old Greek tragedies—viewing the conflict in full knowledge of what has brought it about, knowing more of the circumstances than the actors themselves—yet unlike the onlooker of old, we do not know what will happen. We do not know whether Job will stand the test, whether indeed, as the Adversary suggests, his goodness is but cupboard-love. So Satan has his way; one after another calamity falls upon Job. His sheep, his cattle, his camels, his servants, and finally his sons and daughters are struck down by an appalling series of accidents—lightning, hurricane and marauding bands. But Job bears all this misfortune with remarkable fortitude. He accepts it all as the hand of God. "Naked came I out of my mother's womb, and naked shall I return thither: the Lord gave, and the Lord hath taken away; blessed be the name of the Lord." But Satan is not satisfied. So long as a man's skin is whole, he

can bear anything. "All that a man hath will he give
for his life." Once again, then, the heavenly council
meets. Satan puts his case and is given permission
to harry Job to the point of death. The good man
is smitten with boils from head to foot, a peculiarly
painful type of leprosy called elephantiasis. Modern
treatment promises no cure, even by keeping the
patient in bed with daily injections for three to six
months. Job's treatment—self-administered—was
perforce more rough and ready. "He took him a
potsherd to scrape himself withal and he sat down
among the ashes." His wife gave him little comfort;
her advice was terse: "Curse God and die." Job,
however, denounces this as evil counsel and still
utters no word of reproach against Yahweh. His
three best friends, Eliphaz, Bildad and Zophar,
hear of his plight and hasten to comfort him. But
when they catch sight of him, they are so appalled
that they know at once that no platitudes of consolation will help him. "So they sat down with him
upon the ground seven days and seven nights, and
none spake a word unto him for they saw that his
grief was very great." So ends the prose prologue,
and it is in this setting that we are to imagine the
three acts of the drama—the three cycles of dialogue—taking place.

The rather fanciful picture of the transaction between God and Satan should not obscure the fact
that the poet is here putting forward a serious theory that we must consider in summing up the religious value of the book; namely, that one reason
for the sufferings of good men is to test the quality
of their goodness. It is God's way of finding out

how genuine are men's professions of piety. To be devout and upright when things are going smoothly is easy. But can a man's religion stand up to the buffets of disaster? Here, at least, the author of Job portrays one man who stands the test, the classic case of disinterested goodness. Job is not a picture of a man suffering for his sins but a man chosen by God to prove that in spite of every affliction that flesh is heir to, integrity of mind and sincerity of heart are still a possibility for humankind.

Act I (4–14): Introduction (3), Scene I (4–7)

Each of the three acts consists of six speeches. Job's friends speak in strict rotation, and Job replies to each in turn. The speeches vary in length but are clearly divided in the text. Between the prologue and the first cycle of speeches comes the outburst from Job that sets the drama in motion (chap. 3). As his friends sit silently beside him, the depth of their sympathy and horror at his plight clearly marked by their behavior, Job's composure breaks down. He knows how to answer his wife who tells him bluntly to throw in the sponge. But this silent affection of his friends is too much for him. "He opened his mouth and cursed the day he was born." He does not complain of the injustice of his fate, he utters no accusations against Providence, but as a sick man—sick in mind and body—he prays for death. Why was he ever born? And why is he now denied the peace of the grave? This outburst shocks his friends out of their silence. In what they say, the poet puts the case for the religious orthodoxy of the time against which the whole book is a protest, and Job is the rebel. His friends are convinced from the outset that if a man has sunk to this state of misery and dejection, his afflictions must be merited. God in his justice would not permit anything else. Job was obviously getting no more than he deserved. His passionate outcry was therefore highly improper.

Eliphaz opens the debate (scene 1) in the most tactful manner possible. He is obviously moved by affection for Job. His speech (4–5) is a masterpiece of delicacy. He stresses the *universal, beneficent rule of a wise providence.* The government of the world is in good hands. Job must remember this and not let his own misfortunes dull his remembrance of it. Many another sufferer he has himself comforted; now let him take comfort himself. Men reap what they sow, and no man can be free from guilt. "Man is born unto trouble (i.e., brings trouble on himself) as the sparks fly upward" (5:7). It is the law of life. Surely, then, the wise thing for Job to do is to acknowledge that he has sinned and throw himself on God's mercy. The man who confesses his offense and repents is always sure of pardon. Let Job look on his present ills as a discipline, and things will all come right for him in the end. But this explanation is not good enough for Job. In his reply (chaps. 6–7), he charges Eliphaz with taking too casual a view of his plight. It is all very well for him to talk of the impossibility of avoiding sin against God and therefore of escaping retribution. But surely these sufferings of his are more than most men have to bear, and what great wrong has he done to deserve them? Why ask him to repent when he does not know what to repent of? His friends are of little help to him if that is all they can suggest. Then Job breaks out again (chap. 7) into a desperate cry against the injustice of his lot. Why should God pick upon him? Is he a wild beast who has to be subdued by torture? He parodies bitterly the words of the Psalmist: What is man that God is mindful of him (Ps. 8:4)? He asks what is man that God can't leave him alone, why bother about him, and he calls God the great spy upon mankind.

Act I, Scene 2 (8–10)

Bildad, the second friend, catches on to something Job has said about God's injustice (6:29) and summons up all the weight of human experience against it. He stresses the *discrimination* of God (chap. 8). Job's children obviously sinned, therefore, they were struck down. Job himself cannot have sinned so grossly, otherwise he would have suffered the same fate. Everybody knows this to be true: the good man flourishes, the bad man perishes. Job must start afresh, build up his life anew. If he is as he says without offense, then let him rest assured that if he asks God to bless him, prosperity will return. Job's reply (9–10) is bitterly ironical. Justice there is in God's dealings, but it is the justice of the strong against the weak. Nobody can argue with him. How can a man ever hope to win a case against the Almighty? His justice is what suits himself. Bildad says God discriminates between the good and the bad. Nonsense! Innocent and guilty alike are God's victims just as it pleases him. Providence is not the rule of justice but of universal injustice. If he could only think why it was that God was making him suffer. He looks back on the happiness of his past life—all shattered and gone—and the awful suspicion comes to him that God has perhaps been playing with him like a cat with a mouse. He only raised him up to prosperity in order to enjoy the spectacle of his greater torment. If that is so, then why give him life at all? Now, at any rate, let him have peace. "Are not my days few? Cease then and let me alone that I may take comfort a little, before I go whence I shall not return even to the land of darkness and the shadow of death: a land of darkness as darkness itself and of the shadow of death without any order and where the light is as darkness" (10:20–22). So speaks Job in black despair.

Act I, Scene 3 (11–14)

Eliphaz is the gentlest and most tactful of Job's friends. Bildad is less patient. Zophar is the hardest and narrowest of the three. His reply (chap. 11) to Job begins more abruptly and angrily than the other two. "Can nothing be done to silence this man's babbling and glib talk?" he asks. Job has asked for God to speak and say why he was so tormenting him. If he did speak, the truth would soon be told. Job thinks he is without sin, but God looks deeper than man. The sin is there though Job cannot see it. So let him repent and turn to God, and all will be well. Zophar ends with a stinging reminder about the fate of those who get a chance to repent and don't take it. Job in his answer (12–14) opens with the sarcastic remark, "No doubt but you are the people and wisdom will die with you" (12:2). Zophar's point had been that *God knew everything,* could see deeper than a mere man, could search a man's conscience better than he himself. Job scoffs at this and says the very beasts of the field know that God knows everything. Job certainly doesn't need to be told that—but what is more important than God's universal knowledge is his universal power, and that is what he uses to upset the world as he likes (12:13–25). Job beseeches them not to tell lies in defense of God—not to whitewash God's character—and he asks them to listen while he states his own case more dispassionately than before. He will brave God's displeasure if need be, but he will protest, cost what it may. "He may kill me—what else can I expect—but I will maintain my innocence to his face." So he puts his case before God. Is it worth his while to persecute such a puny thing as a man? "Man that is born of a woman, is of few days and full of trouble" (14:1). Is God not moved by the sadness of human life, its brevity, its pathetic end? If there were only some hope of a life beyond the grave—but even that Job cannot take seriously. The only straw that he can clutch at is that God will allow him to lie hidden in the grave till the inexplicable divine wrath has passed over.

Job's dilemma is an agonizing one. Like his friends, he believes that prosperity rewards a virtuous life and adversity an evil one. But unlike them, he is convinced of his own innocence. His anguish springs from the fact that it seems to him that although God knows he is innocent, he is determined to treat him as if he were guilty. So, while he feels convinced that somehow God is good, he wonders whether his belief is not mistaken, and whether a blind amoral force—indifferent to justice—is not a truer estimate of what rules the universe.

Act II, Scene 1 (15-17)

Job is unconvinced by the arguments of his friends—Eliphaz who talks of God's universal goodness, or Bildad who dwells on his discriminating justice, or Zophar who insists on his omniscient insight. Job is still certain that he does not deserve to suffer. In the second cycle of speeches, the three comforters adopt a second line of argument, not from the nature of God but from the experience of life. Eliphaz opens (chap. 15) rather more sharply than in Act I with the charge that Job, by such wild talk as he has been indulging in, not only offends his friends—men old enough to be his father—but undermines religion itself. As for his accusations of the injustice of things, is it not the case that wicked men suffer agony of mind? The fact of a bad conscience, which Eliphaz describes vividly, is of itself almost punishment enough. Job in reply (16-17) depicts himself as deserted by God and man. His friends' consolation is worse than useless. He appeals to God to justify him and prove his innocence.

Act II, Scene 2 (18–19)

Bildad (18) is piqued at Job's spurning of his friends' advice. He draws an even more drastic picture than Eliphaz of the certain fate that overtakes the wicked in this life. Nothing Job can say will alter the facts of experience: that is what happens, and no one can deny it. It is implicit in what he says that Job is to take these words of comfort to himself. In return, Job (chap. 19) draws the most pitiful picture so far of the fate that has befallen him: persecuted by God, deserted by his friends, loathed by everyone near him. He beseeches his friends to pity him rather than harry him, yet his spirit rises above that to the sublime conviction that God will vindicate him at the last and that even if death befall him here, his innocence will be proved hereafter. This famous passage (19:25–27) shows, like some others in the book of Job and in the Psalms, the growing aspirations of the Hebrew mind for something more adequate than an afterlife consisting of a shadowy existence in Sheol.

Act II, Scene 3 (20–21)

Zophar (20) now repeats more or less the same argument of the other two, that the life of a wicked man is brief. Even if his evil ways bring him prosperity, it is only for a short space; then the vengeance of God comes upon him and destroys him. Job's friends have, of course, been trying to wring from him a confession of guilt. They have depicted the misfortunes of the wicked with the implication that this was what had happened to Job. Twice Job has let it pass with no more than a renewed protest of innocence. This time (chap. 21), he meets it with a challenge of his own; he voices a thought that has been growing within him, a suggestion that makes him tremble to think of it himself. It is no less than what seems to him a denial that there is any moral government in the universe at all: the wicked do not perish—they prosper and grow fat; they are not struck down by the wrath of God—they die in comfort in their beds. This daring assertion of Job, which cuts across the conventions of his time, is of course a truer view of things as they are than the pious statements of his friends. Virtue and vice have nothing to do with a man's prosperity and little to do with his happiness. A self-centered man can be both prosperous and as happy as it is possible for him to be. A man of integrity may be plagued with misfortune and suffer bitterness of spirit. It is not in prosperity or in adversity, in happiness or unhappiness, that the difference between good and bad lies. If prosperity and happiness come, good and well, but "to serve God and love him," as Froude says in his great study of the book of Job, "is higher and better than happiness, though it be with wounded feet and bleeding brow and hearts loaded with sorrow." It is to this faith that Job is steadily rising.

Act III, Scene 1 (22–24)

For the second time Job's friends, exasperated by his obstinate persistence in his innocence, change their ground; they pass from implication to direct accusation. What they do not know as facts they invent. Eliphaz (22) pours out a torrent of abuse, arguing wildly and not even believing it himself but driven—as we are all driven when we feel we are getting worsted—into a position that in a more rational mood he would have scorned. He sees Job's plight and cannot conceive of anything else than that it is the result of sin, so he accuses him outright of inhumanity, of avarice, of oppression. Job is still too absorbed in his new problem of the undoubted prosperity of the wicked to make any reply to the charges (23–24). Blacker and blacker, the more he thinks of it, becomes the realization of how crime goes unpunished.

Act III, Scene 2 (25–27:6)

Note confusion here. Bildad has nothing to say. His arguments are exhausted. He reiterates simply the greatness of God and the imperfection of humanity (25–6). Job replies (27:1–6) by protesting his innocence.

Act III, Scene 3 (27:7–31)

(So far as we can make sense of this part, which is very confused, Zophar seems to repeat the old argument of the fate of the evildoer in 27:7–23). The next chapter, the magnificent poem about Wisdom (28:12–28)—one of the greatest literary gems in the Old Testament (cf. Proverbs 8)—breaks the context, and Job's final answer completing the cycle comes in 29–31. In chapter 29 he looks back upon the good old days of his prosperity, when he was respected and honored. He contrasts this in chapter 30 with his present pitiful state, and in chapter 31 he once more insists that his past life has been blameless. The standard of moral conduct that he sets himself here is as high as anything in the Old Testament. It is part of the argument of the book that this was the kind of behavior expected from a man who claimed to be a good God-fearing Jew, and it is an ideal of which any society anywhere might be proud. It shows, moreover, how deep and lasting an effect the ethical force of the great prophets' teaching had had on society.

Chapters 32–37 are an interpolation. A new speaker, Elihu, comes on the scene. His speech contains little that is fresh. It seems to have been introduced at a later date to enforce the argument that suffering is a moral discipline.

So Job and his friends are silenced; they have exhausted each other by the force of their arguments. His friends are still persuaded that he is guilty of some unknown but heinous sins. Job is just as convinced that he is no more culpable than the common run of men. The great question mark remains: Why, if he has done no wrong, has he to bear this suffering? Job does not doubt at heart that the government of the universe is in wise hands. But the prosperity of wicked men baffles him, as does is his own misfortune. His mind is still perplexed, and nothing his friends have said has helped to solve his problem.

Postlude (38–42:6)

At this point the poet introduces the only person who might give an answer: Yahweh himself. Yahweh's reply is in two parts, each followed by a short speech by Job and with a probable interpolation in 40:15–41:34. "Then Yahweh answered Job out of a whirlwind and said: Who is this that darkeneth counsel by words without knowledge?" (38: 1–2). In magnificent, impressive language, God describes the marvelous intricacy and wonder of the created world (38–39). Job is overwhelmed at the power and majesty and infinite resource of the Creator. He confesses his sin of presumption in wanting to argue with God (40:1–5). Yahweh then asks him (40:6–14) if now he thinks he could make a better job of running the universe than God himself and ironically invites him to try. Job's answer is one of complete penitence—not penitence for his sins, as his friends had demanded, but penitence for questioning the ways of God and for impetuously doubting his providence (42:1–6).

Epilogue (42:7–17)

In the short prose epilogue Yahweh rebukes Job's friends for allowing their conventional orthodoxy to force them into lying arguments. Job is restored to prosperity and lives happily ever after.

Some people have felt that this happy ending is so inappropriate that they have doubted its originality. It seems more likely, however, that the author did not mean Job's new prosperity to be a reward for his unjust suffering but rather suggested that Job, having passed through the fire to a truer view of God's providence and men's fortunes, could now see prosperity as an accidental rather than an essential thing, an adjunct to the good life rather than a necessary part of it. Or it may simply be that the restitution of Job's fortunes was a required vindication in the eyes of the world.

What, then, is the message of the book of Job, and what is its religious value? It must first and foremost be understood as a whole—that is, the prologue is an integral part of it—otherwise it merely states a problem and leaves it unsolved. It must be clear by now that the book offers no hard and fast solution to the problem of undeserved suffering. The author did not intend to. His primary aim was to oppose the current view of his times that rewards and punishments were handed out like prizes in exact correspondence to a man's good or evil deeds. As that is perfectly obvious to us, in this sense the book says nothing new. Its permanent contribution is rather in the picture it gives of a man who loves goodness for its own sake and not for what he can get out of it. He is appalled by the problem set up in his own mind by the inequalities and injustices of life, he is tempted on occasion to question whether there be any Providence at all, but through it all he retains his own integrity. Job might not have been restored to prosperity; he might have died in misery upon his ash heap as many another good man in all ages has done. But if he had, he would still have left a portrait of a man who had realized that the aim of life is not happiness but to hold fast to the good and to scorn the evil. It is only so long as the enjoyment of material prosperity takes first place in a man's mind that the government of the universe seems to be unjust; when it is seen that the highest good in life is to be faithful to God and his laws, then prosperity or adversity becomes a secondary concern. The author of Job in this great book would leave us with the knowledge, despite all insinuations to the contrary—which he personifies as Satan in the prologue—that man is capable of real and disinterested goodness and that he can love God for his own sake without thought of reward. Job has no hope—apart from one or two fleeting aspirations—of a life beyond the grave, and so the quality of his nature is shown up in greater relief. But in his steadfast loyalty to his principles and his complete trust in God, despite every affliction and amid the ruin of his hopes, he touches a height somewhere very near the Cross and inspires us to like service. Job reaches inward peace and the answer to all his problems in the humility of unquestioning trust in God. His martyrdom for the sake of truth forms a new answer for Old Testament thought to the problem of suffering.

The Value and Limitations of the Old Testament

There was a time when it was believed that any attempt to get behind the printed text of the Authorized Version to questions of origin, authenticity, historical value, authorship, etc., was tantamount to sacrilege. People felt that sacred things were being tampered with. Old and dear traditions, the simple faith of childhood, the legacy of pious forebears were thought to be endangered. These tales of reverend patriarchs, King David's role as the Psalmist, King Solomon's as the coiner of Proverbs, together, for some reason or other, with Archbishop Usher's dates, had acquired an almost numinous status in some people's minds, and any interference with them was resented. This older traditional view, compared with the more modern critical approach to the Old Testament, has been likened to two views of a mountain landscape. In the one case, the observer is enraptured with the bold outlines, the rugged grandeur, the blending of color light and shade; in the other, the beholder is a scientist whose interest lies not only in the net effect that the landscape produces but in the geological formations, the mineralogy, the plant life, the bird life, the fossils and all the hundred and one things of interest in any stretch of country. It would be a just criticism of the scientist's point of view if his interest in what lay under the surface diminished his appreciation of the beauty of the scene. Likewise, if our study of the Old Testament leaves us with an impression mainly of minutiae of detail, if the mythical and legendary and unhistorical parts of the text are the things we remember most, then we have clearly got hold of the wrong end of the stick. When the miner finds gold, he lays down his tools, and our whole aim and object in studying the Old Testament critically is to give us better understanding and deeper appreciation of its contents. We should get more out of Isaiah, not less, by knowing that the sixty-six chapters are not written by one man at one time. Moses should be more of a real warrior and statesman for us and less of a plaster saint with a flair for boring legislation. The book of Daniel should no longer be a dubious almanac foretelling future events in an unintelligible way, nor should the book of Jonah be an incredible caricature but a real contribution to the literature of world mission.

This cannot fail to happen if we bring to the study of the Old Testament that one indispensable quality—an open mind. Not a credulous mind but an open mind. Most of the misunderstanding of the Old Testament has been due to the fact that people come to their own conclusions about what it contains before reading it. For some, it is the infallible key to Christian doctrine: for others, a mixture of childish superstition and black magic. As we have,

I hope, discovered, it is neither. But its real value we shall never properly estimate unless we approach it without preconceptions and let it have its own effect upon us. Let us first of all notice some of the most striking characteristics of the nation that produced it.

Characteristics of Israel's history

Its debt to other nations

One thing that has become very patent is that Israel did not live in a vacuum. The Old Testament was not a product of reflection in some sequestered nook but was hammered out in that cockpit of the Middle East, the prey of one great empire after another, where ideas were put to the test not of argument but of experience, and where they were exposed to influences that blew in with the four winds. The religious thought of the Hebrews was no exclusive racial prerogative; it was molded, enhanced and enlarged by contact with their neighbors. We have seen them entering the Promised Land and finding a different religion firmly established there. We have seen how a nomadic people in their transformation into an agricultural people took over not only the secular practices of their new homeland but many of its religious practices as well. The holy places of the baals became the holy places of Yahweh. The festivals and sacrificial ritual of Canaan were adapted to Israel's use. Even the prophets—the glory of Israel's contribution to the world—sprang, so far as we can see, from the order of wandering *Nebiim* already in existence in Palestine. Later on the myths of Babylon gave Israel its framework for the explanation of the Creation and the other prehistoric events in the early chapters of Genesis. Later still Persian influence can be seen in the growth of the idea of an intermediate angelic host between God and man and in the increasingly independent role of Satan. In the department of law, the Code of Hammurabi of Babylon has clearly made its mark upon the Mosaic legislation. How much of this foreign influence in general was direct, that is, consciously borrowed, and how much was indirect, that is, unconsciously assimilated or drawn from a common source, is a matter of conjecture. But clearly it is a fact to be reckoned with.

Its great personalities

It must strike everyone that one of the salient characteristics in the history of Israel is the astonishing number of notable men it produced. There was no Golden Age of Pericles, or Augustan, or Elizabethan heyday—the whole history is a heyday. One after another in steady succession appear men —Moses, Elijah, Isaiah, Nehemiah—whose greatness is manifest even on the tiny stage on which they played, men who were not merely men of God or molders of history but both combined. And the achievement of others, such as Amos, Hosea, Ezekiel and Isaiah of Babylon, was to shape the religious ideas of the nation and raise them to a pitch that no other group of thinkers in any other country ever aspired to. Israel's small stage offered plenty of scope for the initiative of individual men of thought and action. Such men did not merely slavishly accept what elements came to them from other lands; they took them over, assimilated them and enriched them, so that the end result of all Israel's foreign influences was that they absorbed the best elements from outside sources and modified them in the best way.

Its unique self-consciousness

No other people has ever had such a sense of superiority, exclusiveness and national pride as the Hebrews. They were the Chosen People. The name still sticks to them though now as a wry jest. At its worst, it could be racial narrowness of the worst kind, at its best it was a deep consciousness of a unique national vocation. They felt they were the People of God in a very real sense, not for what they could get out of it, but for whom God had chosen to reveal his nature and purpose to the world. This sense of their own destiny as bearers of divine truth to the world was something that never left them. However primitive their conception of Yahweh at one time had been, in its fullest development it was as Ruler and Creator of the world. Was it effrontery or nationalist bigotry for this tiny pocket edition of a nation to conceive of its role as messengers of this universal God, as the enlighteners of the world, or was it the truth? History surely gives the answer. If the Hebrews were wrong, the whole of Christianity is a delusion.

The purpose running through it all

We cannot have come so far in studying the course of Israel's history without being struck by the sense of a purpose running through the whole course of events. It is not merely that Israel itself had this consciousness but that we as outside observers are constrained to admit it. Through the clash of empires, the rise and fall of Israel as a state, the disasters and mischances that befell its people, grew steadily the most lofty religious beliefs of the ancient world. Political events contributed to them; so did the personalities of kings and leaders. And on this tiny stage are exhibited progressively all the crucial issues that affect man's religious life. Surely it was no sequence of accidents or flukes that produced this ever-widening horizon, this deepening insight into the mystery that lies at the center of life.

Let us pause, now, to consider some of the limitations of the Old Testament. Perhaps limitations is not the proper word. It suggests such obvious things as the juxtaposition of psalms that tell of the majesty of God and psalms that pray for infants to be dashed to death, of prudential morality side by side with the loftiest ethical teaching, of historical inaccuracies and primitive science. On a reasonable view of Scripture, however, as a progressive development of ideas, as a literary deposit of many centuries, and as primarily a storehouse of religious and not scientific or historical facts, objections such as these lose most of their point. We do not expect to find in the Old Testament, knowing its structure and composition, a level surface of equal moral and religious insight, but growth and progress, survivals and anachronisms, inaccuracy of detail and human fallibility. What is more important is to notice what is perhaps better called the Old Testament's inconclusiveness.

Inconclusiveness of the Old Testament

The Old Testament leaves many problems unsolved and hands them on to the New Testament for solution so far as any solution can be given. Some of these problems arose through the march of events, some through the inevitable circumscribing of Old Testament religion by its own presuppositions, some through the tension of trying to realize in ordinary life the extraordinarily high standards that the prophets of Israel sought to establish.

Public versus private religion

The priests insisted that religion was an affair of the temple, of sacrifice, of ritual; the prophets insisted that it was a matter of individual rectitude and piety. Here was a tension that still exists between the conception of religion as churchgoing and as a man's own private relationship with God. The problem seemed to be solved by a growing emphasis on the part of the priesthood upon prayer rather than ritual, but it was merely a change of position, because it became more and more the practice of laymen who claimed to be godly to fill their lives with the punctilious observance of details of the Law—witness the Pharisees of New Testament times. So one set of external observances was replaced by another, much as the Puritans of post-Reformation days replaced the ritual of Roman Catholic sacramentalism with the ritual of Sabbath Observance. It was left to Jesus to clear the air.

Universal versus national religion

The prophets had not spoken with one voice upon this subject. Isaiah of Babylon and Ezekiel—the last two of the great galaxy—had put forward opposing views. Despite such protesters as Ruth and Jonah, nationalism prevailed. As C. H. Dodd points out in *The Authority of the Bible,* it is a difficulty that can hardly be avoided. The patriot who is also a religious man wants his country to be God's own country, goes on to believe it such and ends with "So let thine enemies perish Lord." It is a problem for every age to reconcile the natural patriotism of man—however religious—with his knowledge that at heart all men are brothers. The Old Testament could not solve it and passed it on to the New.

Is God near us or far away?

The old Israelite had an easy answer to this question. God was incomprehensible, but he lived in very comprehensible surroundings—trees, rivers, mountains, the Ark of the Covenant. Then the prophets swept away all the homely evidences of Yahweh's presence, insisting on his majesty and power. For them it was easy to reconcile the two—their own personal consciousness of God made him seem very near to them despite his remote holiness.

But for the average man, this reconciliation was not easy. Hence along one line the elaboration of ritual in approaching the temple: God dwelt there but must be surrounded with all the paraphernalia of inapproachability. Hence, too, the growth of belief in angels, or Wisdom (as in Prov. 8 and Job 28), as intermediaries who make known God's will to men. This problem, too, remained unanswered.

The injustices of life

We have gone into this pretty thoroughly already, so all that need be done here is to note that the suffering of the innocent man was one of the greatest worries for the Old Testament thinker who maintained that God was just and that the universe was run on beneficent lines.

The life beyond

This issue, too, can be briefly dealt with. Most of the Old Testament moves on the plane of this world. Never does the thought of any life beyond bulk largely in the mind of Israel. An odd Psalm (73) and the book of Job hint at it rather than express it. Yet the whole tendency of Old Testament religion based upon a deep and enduring relationship with God is pointing in that direction. It is a tension that only the New Testament could tackle. Finally, let us try to summarize the Old Testament's permanent value.

Permanent value of the Old Testament

At a course of lectures for school chaplains that I once attended, one of the chaplains spoke of the difficulty he found in answering questions his young son put to him about the Old Testament. The boy, for example, asked why the Israelites were always having to fight the Hittites, the Amorites, the Canaanites, the Perizzites, etc. His father replied that the Israelites wanted to occupy their country. To which the boy said: Just like Hitler. The father added—at the conference—that to almost every question that the boy asked, the answer had to be: You can't understand that without the New Testament. And the father's point was: What's the use of teaching the Old Testament at all? The same reflection must cross people's minds when in church some particularly dull or barbarous passage is read as the Old Testament lesson. Taken out of its context, there does not seem to be much inspiration in an incident such as Samuel's hewing Agag in pieces before the Lord, or the description of Jezebel's corpse being worried by the town mongrels until all that was left was the skull and the feet and the palms of her hands, to say nothing of some of the dreary stretches of Mosaic legislation. The answer to both these problems is, of course, selection. Parts of the Old Testament are obviously neither suitable for teaching to children nor for reading in church. Children should not be taught anything out of the Bible that does not harmonize with the life and teaching of Jesus, or learn primitive ideas about God that they will find difficult to get rid of, and no Old Testament lesson should be given the same place in a church service as a New Testament lesson unless it is of New Testament caliber of thought and morality. But having made these qualifications, and having added that *(a)* the Old Testament background must be known before the text is understood and *(b)* the Authorized Version or Revised Version should be read in conjunction with a modern translation like the New English Bible or a commentary of some sort, how are we to assess its permanent value for the private, adult reader?

One of the Old Testament stories tells of a dead man whose body came to life again when it was thrown into the grave of a prophet. That is perhaps a parable, for it is as much as anything because of the deathlessness of the prophets that the Old Testament is still a living force in the world today.

The prophets

The prophets of Israel were in one sense religious geniuses, and genius is both international and eternal. As Shakespeare, Dante and Goethe transcend the limitations of their age and environment and speak to our times as much as to their own; as Michelangelo, Dürer and Leonardo reproduce a beauty that is not Italian or German Renaissance but eternal; or as Beethoven, Bach and Brahms have the universal appeal and significance of men who have heard greater than human harmonies, so Isaiah, Amos, Hosea, Jeremiah—time-conditioned men of Israel though they were—are the means whereby we are able as nowhere else to glimpse the eternal values of goodness, justice, mercy and truth that lie at the heart of the universe. Isaiah's vision of God, Hosea's sense of his love, Amos' perception of his justice were so real and unmistakable that they become real for us too. Through the prophets' consciousness of religious truth, our own convictions are strengthened and our spirits are attuned to theirs in acknowledging that their interpretation of God is just and true.

Psalms

Here is an imperishable storehouse of the ingredients of religion for the ordinary man. More than a hymnbook, the Psalter strikes every note of human emotion. Here is comfort for the man in despair, praise for his jubilation, guidance for his perplexity. The book of Psalms is permeated by such a sense of the reality of God, his nearness, his holiness, his compassion and his majesty, that no one who reads it can fail to find something for his own needs. And what of the Wisdom Literature?

Wisdom Literature

The wrestling of a tortured soul in the book of Job finding release and an answer at last, the frank realism of Ecclesiastes who will not be put off with easy comfort, or the best of the ethical teaching of the Proverbs: these things are immortal whether they are found in Greece, Rome or Israel.

Primitive tales

It is perhaps not so clear to us at first sight what permanent value lies in the lowest stratum of the

Old Testament stories—the level of primitive religion we see in, for example, Jacob's struggle with the river god or Moses and the burning bush. But tales like these have their value on two levels. There is the value of the finished work—the story as it is related by the Hebrew historians—told in the light of later and wider understanding of the nature of religion. What was once a pagan belief in gods of hill and mountain and stream has now become the medium of expressing the mental struggle between the old deceitful man that was Jacob and the promptings of God, ending in Jacob's conversion and rebirth as a new man, Israel (Gen. 32:22–32). Or in the story of the burning bush it is not as a primitive superstition that Yahweh was a god of fire that the writer of Exodus recounts it, but as the characteristic of God that he is a living fire in the world, giving light, power, inspiration, kindling men's hearts but not destroying them. Before this holy fire Moses does homage, for he is on holy ground. Most of these ancient tales based on the earliest type of religious belief can be thus seen to be of a twofold character: one, the primitive foundation that lies behind it, and two, the religious interpretation that the compiler means it to have. Even the primitive substructure has a permanent value, however, because beneath the veneer of civilization and such religious faith as we have, the primitive animist within us is not yet dead. We still have the grisly, creepy sense of the numinous that the savage had though we fight it down or tell ourselves that it is nonsense; we still are at heart superstitious pagans, credulous and impressionable like the ancient Hebrews. And it anchors us firmly to the solid earth to feel that it is out of these unconfessed, undeveloped traces of a primitive stage of life that we recognize at odd moments within ourselves that the sublime flower of Old Testament religion at its highest sprang into life. There is another aspect of these old tales that is worth noting and that gives them permanent value from another angle; that is that they portray the inward side of apparently external movements. One of the recurrent features of human history is the restlessness of virile races; we call it economic necessity and put it down to the need for more food or wider markets. Here in the Old Testament we see two such migrations in action: the Abraham tribes from Ur of the Chaldees to Palestine, and the Israelites under Moses from Egypt to their Promised Land. In both cases we see them from the inside—we see how, as well as being influenced by things like famine, men are moved by the lust for adventure, by a spiritual restlessness that cannot be equated with economic necessity. The Old Testament is a salutary antidote in this respect to the barren concept of economic man and gives us a truer picture of his nature and destiny, telling us that this discontent with things as they are is a divine prompting that can be brought into harmony with the purposes of God.

Looking at the Old Testament as a whole, can we single out certain aspects of its permanent value?

Literary value

Most people would put the literary value of the Old Testament first because it is the most obvious. Whether the Old Testament is regarded as a revelation of the will and purpose of God, or whether it is looked on as a collection of ancient fairy tales, the one thing that no one disputes is its abiding value as literature. But however great that value may be, it is clear that whatever else the Old Testament was, it was not designed to be read as literature, and in fact its literary worth is the least of all its claims on our attention. So in putting it first here, it is with the intention of leading up from the more obvious to the less obvious, but at the same time from the least valuable to the most valuable.

Human value

Surely more than being merely a handbook to literary style the Old Testament is a handbook to something more vital—the study of human nature. Our fellow men are after all our deepest interest—not politics, not theories, but mankind. And where is there a greater range of human interest than in the Old Testament—where is there a more widely assorted collection of saints and scoundrels, rich and poor, wise and foolish? There are men and women there to whom any man alive would doff his hat, and there are others whose vileness shames their humanity. There are no rose-colored spectacles worn by the Old Testament writers—they see men and women as they are, not as they might be —and the glory of it all is that it is through these very mortal creatures, with all their failings and frailties, their greatness and their meanness, that the divine spirit is seen at work. Robust playboys appear, like Samson, David of the big heart, Solomon the ostentatious, Absalom the vain. Sweet little Ruth and scheming mother-in-law Naomi cast their net round honest Boaz. Bumptious Haman enraged over dour Mordecai gets hoist with his own petard. These and many more live. They are people we know, described with the sure pen of men who read not only faces but the minds that lie behind. This is perhaps the real value of the historical section of the Old Testament. *When* Solomon reigned or the kingdom divided is a matter of little importance; the historian will find more accurate history for what it is worth in the archaeological discoveries among Israel's neighbors. But the ordinary man will always respond to the ideal friendship of David and Jonathan, to Micaiah's stand for the truth against the 400 false prophets, to Nehemiah's bold rebuilding of the wall despite all opposition.

Moral value

A stage higher than the permanent human interest of the Old Testament lies its moral emphasis. There is no literature of the ancient world with an accent on morality in any way comparable. From the most dim beginnings, life is conceived as being a matter of obligations, duties and responsibilities. History is interpreted on moral lines: the worship of God is seen to be bound up with moral conduct. Whether it is Moses drawing up the Covenant, or

Nathan challenging David about Bathsheba, or Elijah challenging Ahab about Naboth's vineyard, or later the great utterances of the prophets on the true service of God, the same note occurs again and again—justice, goodness, mercy, truth. These are the things that matter in life, not money and social success.

Religious value

Perhaps the greatest difficulty in assessing the value of the religious ideas of the Old Testament lies in their familiarity. In the process of tracing the development of the ideas of the Hebrews, we find at the end not something new but something we have known all along. We found that the developed ideas of the Old Testament on God portrayed him as Creator of the universe, Ruler of men's lives, controlling and directing the world toward the realization of his purposes. Man, we found, was conceived of as wholly dependent upon God for all that he has and is, owing him the service of obedience to his laws and capable of entering into the deepest fellowship with him. The very fact that these conclusions are now almost commonplace is an indication itself of their abiding value. It is because men since Old Testament days have found these answers to correspond so closely with their own reflection and experience that they stand on their own feet. With little change in substance, they were taken over into Christianity. Jesus does not elaborate proofs of God or embark upon exhaustive enquiry into any of these other topics, he assumes them all and incorporates them in his gospel.

This is not to say that the New Testament adds nothing to the Old—far from it—but it does mean that freed from the necessary limitations of nationalism and Jewish religious observances, the substance of these ideas was such as could with little alteration be accepted as the foundation stones of Christianity.

Revelational value

This brings us to the last and highest value of the Old Testament—namely, that it is part of God's unique revelation to man. A word on revelation. Most of our emphasis—being human—lies upon our discoveries about God. But if God is Personality and not a blind cosmic force, we can only discover what he chooses to reveal. Ultimately man's quest for God and God's quest for man are two sides of the same coin—the process is a double one. We have talked of the growing insight of the Hebrews into the nature and being of God and his will for men. We might with equal truth have spoken of God's gradual revelation of himself and his purposes to the Hebrews. From this point of view, God revealed himself to Israel through the chances and changes of their national fortunes—calling Abraham from among the Chaldees, prompting Moses to lead the people out of Egypt and to establish the Covenant as the foundation of the relationship between Israel and their God, speaking to the nation at divers times through prophets and thinkers, sowing the seed, preparing the way until in the fullness of time he gave his final revelation of himself in Jesus Christ. We have spoken of the inconclusiveness of the Old Testament—that is its inevitable characteristic, for it is the prelude to the New. Time after time in our study of the New Testament, we shall find not only that Christianity builds upon the Old Testament but that Christianity cannot be understood apart from it. Old and New Testaments are inseparable parts of one whole—God's disclosure of himself, his nature and his purpose, to humanity. There is no finality in the Old Testament. It leaves us with many loose ends that can only be tied up in the New. It finishes with a large question mark, to which the answer can only be given in Jesus Christ.

BOOK 2

The Gospels: The Heart of the New Testament

Matthew

The gospel that stands first in our New Testament was by far the most popular in the early Church. Matthew's was *the* gospel par excellence. This is not surprising, for among other characteristics that would endear it particularly to the first few generations of Christians is the fact that no gospel links up so closely the Old Testament with the New Testament. It is indeed the most proper bridge between the Testaments, for its emphasis throughout is on the fact that in Jesus all the hopes and promises of Israel have been fulfilled. He is the Messiah of whom all the prophets spoke, and he has brought into being a New Israel—no longer limited to one nation—but a Kingdom as wide as the universe.

The first thing that must be said about this gospel is that as it stands it is clearly not the work of Matthew the disciple, for it is nothing more or less than a revised and enlarged edition of Mark. It would be a most extraordinary thing if a man who had been in the closest possible association with Jesus should be content to relate incidents of his ministry in the exact words of another man who was a very secondary witness. Almost all of Mark's book is to be found reproduced, sometimes verbatim, by Matthew (approximately 600 verses out of 661). But more interesting than the correspondence are the alterations he makes. Using Mark as his basis, this unknown author rearranges, amends and omits in a way that indicates that he is not prepared to accept Mark as the last word but has his own ideas on the subject. It is worth noticing what he does.

Mark's gospel is notoriously candid. It not only has a rare vividness and realism, but it has also a certain bluntness that may well be derived from Peter the Galilean fisherman, whose reminiscences lie behind it. Jesus and the disciples appear very human in their emotions and reactions. It is one of the guarantees of the authentic note of the earliest tradition. It is not that Jesus is portrayed as merely a man—far from it. What C. H. Dodd calls the "mysterious undercurrent" is felt throughout the gospel, but the predominant impression that is left by Mark is the reality of our Lord's humanity. Here was a man of real flesh and blood who felt anger, surprise, weariness, astonishment; who could not always achieve what he wanted to do. In other words, in Mark we sense the reality of the Incarnation—Jesus did not *appear* to be a man, he *was* a man, and that was the first impact his personality made upon the disciples. It was their gradual realization as they lived with him and watched him that he was something more that grew in time into the Christian creeds.

Now Matthew, writing later than Mark, and without the salutary corrective of Peter's memory, is afraid that this realistic treatment of Jesus will be misunderstood, and so he either waters down or omits anything that looks like disparaging Jesus. Jesus must not be violently moved, whether by anger, compassion or indignation (cf. Mk. 3:5 with Matt. 12:9–14; Mk. 1:41 with Matt. 8:3–4; Mk. 10:14 with Matt. 19:14). He will not have it that there were some things that Jesus could not do— enter a city, or perform a miracle, or conceal himself, or destroy and rebuild the temple (e.g., Mk. 1:45, 6:5, 7:24, 14:58)—or that there was anything he did not know—such as the name of the man possessed of evil spirits, or who touched him in a crowd, or the number of loaves available for feeding the multitude (e.g., Mk. 5:9–30, 6:38). In all these cases Matthew amends slightly or simply leaves out what he regards as Mark's dangerous frankness. In other cases he makes significant alterations: e.g., Mk. 10:18, "Why callest thou me good?" Matt. 19:17, "Why askest thou me concerning that which is good?" Mk. 6:3, "Is not this the carpenter?" Matt. 13:55, "Is not this the carpenter's son?" The forthrightness of Mark, Matthew feels, endangers Jesus' divinity. Similarly the disciples must be protected from misunderstandings, and Mark's slightly irreverent treatment of them must be corrected—they must not need to be rebuked for stupidity or cowardice by Jesus. Instead of being amazed at the stilling of the sea, they must be portrayed worshiping him as the Son of God (cf. Mk. 4:13; Matt. 13:16–17; Mk. 4:40; Matt. 8:26; Mk. 6:52; Matt. 14:33). James and John must not be shown up squabbling for places in the

Messiah's kingdom (Mk. 10:35), so Matthew puts the blame on their mother and makes her do the asking (Matt. 20:20).

So far, then, we have considered one ingredient of Matthew's gospel, namely Mark, and have noted how he has manipulated it. But besides Mark there are three other ingredients, constituting the enlargement we spoke of. The first of these is Q, a common source available to the writing of Synoptic gospels. Matthew's version of the teaching of Jesus is found in five great discourses, the best known of which is the Sermon on the Mount (5–7); the other four are chapters 10, 13, 18 and 24–25. It is clear that this grouping is not accidental, because the whole gospel falls naturally into five sections, each consisting of narrative followed by discourse, (1) 3–4, 5–7, (2) 8–9, 10, (3) 11–12, 13, (4) 14–17, 18, (5) 19–22, 23–25, plus a prologue and an epilogue and each ending with the same formula (7: 28, 11:1, 13:53, 19:1, 26:1). It looks as though Matthew wanted his gospel to suggest that the five books of the Law of Jesus now superseded the five books of the Law of Moses. In his arrangement of Q, the author of Matthew has again acted arbitrarily. He is not concerned with the chronological order of Jesus' teaching but is bent on grouping it together in accordance with subject matter, whether it comes from Q, Mark or elsewhere. This desire for orderliness of arrangement, however, means that we get a better idea of the original Q from Luke, who has no such passion for tidiness and probably more respect for when a certain saying was uttered. Incidentally, the same tendency in dealing with the incidents in Mark's gospel suggests that if we want to know the order of events in Jesus' life, we had better not rely too much on Matthew. People with a mathematical turn of mind will be intrigued to find that he is more interested in his grouping of incidents, facts and persons, or sayings in sequences of threes, fives or sevens, than in following Mark's order: for example, three miracles of healing—the leper, the centurion's servant, Peter's mother-in-law (8:1–17)—three miracles of power—over the storm, over demons, over paralysis (8:23–9:7)—three miracles of restoration—of life, of sight and of speech (9:18–33). Chapter 23 is full of triplets—scribes, Pharisees, hypocrites (23:13)—feasts, synagogues, market places (23: 6–7)—mint, anise, cummin—judgment, mercy, faith (23:23). Parables and woes occur in sevens (chaps. 13 and 23). This was possibly to enable them to be more easily remembered.

The third element in Matthew's gospel is very much in harmony with the whole emphasis on Jesus as the fulfillment of prophecy. This consists of the introduction of a series of texts from the Old Testament—eleven in number—all of which are designed to prove that the events of Jesus' life happened exactly in accordance with Old Testament expectations of the Messiah or that there is close parallelism between some incident in his life and some Old Testament reference. Not all of them strike us as particularly apt (e.g., it is difficult to know what he means by seeing Jesus' home at Nazareth as a fulfillment of prophecy since the prophets do not connect the Messiah with Nazareth and Jesus was certainly not a Nazirite [2:23], and the analogy between Israel being delivered out of Egypt [Hos. 11:1] and the Holy Family returning from there after Herod's massacre of the infants [Matt. 2:15] is rather farfetched), but they are interesting for the light they shed upon the methods of Jewish Christians in the early Church in presenting the gospel to their countrymen, and they indicate the important place given to the Old Testament in missionary circles. It is thought that these texts (Matt. 1:22, 2:5, 15, 17, 23, 4:14, 8:17, 12:17, 13:35, 21:4, 27:9) must come from some book of Testimonies such as are believed to have been used by the Church rather than from the Bible itself. This source would seem to be indicated by the fact that Matthew slips up twice in quoting his authority: the text in 27:9 is from Zechariah 11:13, not Jeremiah, and the one in 13:35 is from a psalmist (78:2), not a prophet. In a book of Testimonies, the author's name would not be given each time.

Lastly there is a fair quantity of material in this gospel that is found nowhere else. This material, like Luke's special source of information, consists of both narratives and teaching and was presumably tradition in circulation in the Church to which Matthew belonged. The teaching consists of parts of the five discourses not found in Luke, and therefore possibly not from Q, parables like the tares, the unforgiving servant, the laborers, the ten virgins, the sheep and the goats and some odd sayings. It is characteristic of this special Matthew material that it is here that a specifically Jewish note appears most strongly (e.g., 10:5–6, 10:23, 6:17–20, 23:2–3).

Among the narratives found only in Matthew are the nativity and childhood stories (chaps. 1 and 2), Peter walking on the water (14:28–31), the coin in the fish's mouth (17:24–27), and, in the Passion story (26–28), the incidents of Judas and the thirty pieces of silver, Judas hanging himself, Pilate's wife's dream, Pilate washing his hands, the earthquake and resurrection of the saints, the watch on the tomb, the angel rolling away the stone and the bribing of the guard.

Who was the author?

As we have seen, whoever the author was it is unlikely that he was the apostle Matthew, and indeed the author is unknown. Yet Matthew's name has always been associated with this gospel. Why is this? Bishop Papias (*c.* A.D. 60–135) supplies the answer. His observation is as follows: "So then Matthew composed the oracles (logia) in the Hebrew language and each one interpreted them as he could." Some think this refers to a collection of proof texts on which Matthew certainly draws more than any other gospel; others—and this seems more likely—think that "logia" refers to the sayings of Jesus, and that very probably the apostle Matthew did make the collection of teaching that we now call Q. Later when the unknown author of the first gospel drew so largely on Q for his material, the name of Matthew came to be attached to the whole work. Whoever he was, this unknown evangelist tells us a little about himself without intending to. His gospel reveals him as a Christian Jew living in the culture that developed within his call following its dispersal, as a result of conquest, throughout the ancient world. His aim is clearly to commend Jesus, to those of his countrymen who were increasingly opposed to Christianity, on the grounds that here at last is the crown of the whole Old Testament structure. But he is still very much a Jew himself— his thinking is Jewish and so are his interests. The place of writing may well have been Antioch since Q is thought to have originated there, and Ignatius, bishop of Antioch, speaks of Matthew as apparently the only gospel he knows at the beginning of the second century. Its date is somewhere in the third quarter of the first century—after Mark (65), on which it draws, and before Clement of Rome (96), who quotes it. Possibly it was written about 80–85.

Characteristics

In addition to the more superficial characteristics of this gospel that we have already noted, namely, the author's love of orderly arrangement at the expense of chronological sequence, his corrections and amendments to Mark's version, and his love of numerical aids to memory, it may be worthwhile to notice some other features that go much deeper. Firstly, of course, there is the fact that this is clearly the *gospel for the Jews* just as Luke's is the gospel for the Gentiles. The keynote is that Jesus is the Messiah for whom the Jews have been waiting. Matthew calls Jesus Son of David eight times as against Mark's twice. In the first verses of the gospel (1: 1–17), there is a curious piece of artificial juggling

with history and mathematics that is designed to
prove that as there were fourteen generations from
Abraham to David, the same number from David
to the Exile, and again from then to Jesus, and since
the letters of David's name in Hebrew are the
equivalent of fourteen in numerals, therefore Jesus
is the Messiah. From that point right through the
gospel Matthew traces step by step the way in
which Jesus fulfills all that the prophets had foretold
and Israel had expected. Born in Bethlehem, the
city of David, worshiped by the Gentile kings, fore-
shadowed by the last and greatest of the prophets,
John the Baptist, the Messiah had come, bringing
a New Law, establishing a New Covenant and
founding a New Israel. It was Matthew's task to
combine the old Jewish belief in the privileges of
their unique relationship to God with the universalism of Christianity that embraced Jew and Gentile
alike. He does this by regarding Israel of old as the
historical predecessor of the Christian Church. This
interest in the Church that appears in certain passages
peculiar to Matthew may be called a second characteristic. There are, for example, the sayings of Jesus
in 28:19–20 and 8:17ff., all of them penetrating to
the very heart of the Christian faith. There is also
the notable promise to Peter in 16:18 ff. on which
the Roman Church builds so much of its claim. A
third characteristic is Matthew's interest in *apocalyp-
ticism.* It may be that his gospel was written at a time
when the Nero-redivivus myth had turned men's
minds again to thoughts of antichrist (24:15), or it
may have been that many were disappointed because the fall of Jerusalem had not ushered in the

cataclysmic kingdom. At all events references to the last things and the return of Christ are rife, for example, 25:13, 25:31, 24:14, 24:42. Lastly there is a *heightening of the miraculous* element. Where Mark makes Jesus heal the sick who crowded round the door (1:32–34), Matthew (8:16) records that he healed them just "with a word"; where the multitudes are fed (Mk. 6:44, 8:9), their number is increased by women and children (Matt. 14:21, 15:38); where the fig tree is cursed (Mk. 11:14–20), it withers immediately (Matt. 21:19). In Matthew's special material, it is noteworthy how many of the incidents are miraculous—Peter walking on the water (14:28–31), the earthquake and rising of the saints at the Crucifixion (27:51–53), the angel who rolls away the stone from the tomb (28:2–4).

Historical value of Matthew

It is generally agreed that the narrative material peculiar to Matthew is of least value in arriving at a true picture of Jesus' ministry. Much of it may be special pleading and apologetic, and no doubt some of Matthew's miracles approach the borderline of the apocryphal gospels and serve mainly to show up more clearly the value of Mark and Luke. As a repository of the teaching of Jesus, however, Matthew is invaluable. Not the least useful function of criticism is that it enables us to discriminate between the different strata that go to make up the gospels. If we are perplexed by some passage or incident that does not seem to harmonize with the spirit of the gospels as a whole, it is often a guide to its accuracy to enquire in which source it appears.

Note

The general view held by New Testament scholars today is that the first three gospels—Matthew, Mark and Luke—are based on two primary sources: Mark's own gospel, consisting mainly of narrative, and a second source consisting mainly of Jesus' teaching, called for convenience Q. The gospels of Matthew and Luke are made up of these two sources, but each of them has in addition special material peculiar to itself, presumably derived from the Church communities in which these gospels were written.

Mark

It was a convention of early sculptors and painters to associate the four gospels with the four faces of the cherubim in Ezekiel's vision (Ezek. chap. I). Either the different gospel writers were represented as a man, a lion, an ox and an eagle, or else these features were included in the same work of art. Matthew is usually the man—sometimes an angel—Mark is the lion, Luke is the ox and John is the eagle. Whether the original idea was to suggest the characteristic tone of the different gospels or not, this identification with the animals of Ezekiel does serve to bring out two points worth noting: first, the gospels differ in character and emphasis, and second, they are nevertheless the same gospel. One interpretation of the animals is that Matthew's gospel represents the kingly character of Christ (the angel), Mark's stresses his power (the lion), St. Luke's lays weight on his sacrifice (the ox), while John's (the eagle) is the heavenly soaring gospel. Another idea along different lines is that the four gospels give us pictures of a past, present, future and ever-present Lord. Matthew shows Christ's relation to the Old Testament, Mark depicts him as active in history, the Jesus of Luke's gospel is the Christ who supplies the needs of all humanity and fulfills all their hopes, while John portrays the eternal Son of God incarnate. These characteristics, which, though true in a general sense, cannot be pressed too far, point to the fact that the individuality of each gospel writer is apparent. Each gives to a certain extent a different aspect of Jesus, each is directed to meet slightly different situations and to interpret Christ to different circles of readers. But this must not lead us to think that there are four different gospels. There is only one gospel presented by four writers, one Christ as seen by four disciples. The correct title of the gospels needs always to be stressed. It is not the gospels *of* Matthew, Mark, Luke and John, but the Gospel or Good News of Jesus Christ *according to* Matthew, Mark, Luke and John. Originally there were no authors' names attached at all. The first verse of St. Mark's little book, "The beginning of the gospel of Jesus Christ the Son of God," is important, because that is how it was first regarded.

When Mark, who is by general agreement the earliest of the four evangelists, wrote these words, he was creating unwittingly a new type of literature. Justin Martyr, one of the early Church fathers, could not find a better name for the gospels than "memoirs." But they are like no memoirs that we know of. The characteristic of classical memoirs— for example, Xenophon's *Memorabilia* (of Socrates) —is that their author lets it be known at once who he is, what his acquaintance with the subject of his book has been, or what his authority is for taking the matter in hand at all. There is nothing of this in the gospels. The personalities of the writers are never obtruded—indeed they are hardly even mentioned. The characteristic that strikes us first is their anonymity. If it were not for sources of information outside their gospels, we should know nothing about them. They at any rate are quite clear that what they are writing is Good News about the Son of God and not casual gossip about some departed worthy. For the same reason we cannot call the gospels biographies of Jesus. They lack all the ordinary features that would entitle them to be classed as such. They give certainly an outline of his life, and it proceeds in a reasonably orderly and chronological way—but of the personal appearance of Jesus, his background, his boyhood and early manhood we know little or nothing. The interest of the writers throughout is on another plane: they are writing Good News from God where what matters is the mighty acts that Jesus did and the words he said, and not the kind of humdrum details that apply to ordinary mortals.

Who wrote it?

Who then was the anonymous creator of this new type of literature that we call a gospel? As he does not tell us himself, we must fall back on tradition, but in this case tradition is unanimous that the author was John Mark, not one of the twelve disciples himself but closely associated with the most notable of them, St. Peter. Let us recall the famous fragment of Papias, the second-century bishop of

Hierapolis in Phrygia. In it he quotes the Presbyter John—contemporary with Mark—as saying, "Mark indeed who had formerly been the interpreter of Peter wrote accurately as far as he remembered them, the things said or done by the Lord, but not however in order. For he had neither heard the Lord nor been his personal follower, but at a later stage, as I said, he had followed Peter, who used to adapt the teachings to the needs (of the moment) but not as though he were drawing up a connected account of the oracles of the Lord: so that Mark committed no error in writing certain matters just as he remembered them. For he had one object only in view, viz. to leave out nothing of the things which he had heard and to include no false statement among them." It is not quite clear what Papias means by "interpreter." Does it mean that Peter spoke only Aramaic and had to be interpreted by the Greek-speaking Mark when talking to Gentiles? Against this it may be said that Galilee was a fairly cosmopolitan place, and Jesus and the disciples may well have been bilingual. Jesus, for example, talks to a Syro-Phoenician woman and to Pilate, presumably in both cases in Greek, and Peter may have shared this ability. At all events Mark's association with Peter is well established, and it is owing to that no doubt that later on both Matthew and Luke use Mark as a foundation for their own gospels.

As it happened the heyday of Mark's gospel was short lived. It was felt by the early Church that the gospels of Matthew and Luke were not only longer and fuller but better, and that of Mark was rather a poor, crude first attempt. From our point of view, however, it is in one respect more valuable than either in that it takes us one stage nearer the great events in Galilee and Jerusalem. Another observation of Papias is open to question. He says that Mark had neither heard the Lord nor been his personal follower. This statement is no doubt true in the sense that Mark was not a disciple of Jesus, but it is highly probable that he had both seen Jesus and been with him at least in the week that ended on Calvary. Indeed there is a fair amount of information in the New Testament—particularly in the Book of Acts—that enables us to form some idea of his background and career, and one incident in his gospel suggests at least that his knowledge of Passion Week was not secondhand.

Mark first appears in the New Testament in Acts 12:12 where he is referred to as John, whose other name was Mark. In the next chapter (verse 5), he is called John, but gradually his name seems to have changed from the Jewish first name to the Latin second name, and after chapter 15 he is simply called Mark. He was the son of Mary, apparently a well-to-do matron in Jerusalem (12:12); whether a widow or not is unknown. We hear nothing of the father, but we know that Mark was a cousin of Barnabas, the great friend of Paul (Col. 4:10). His mother must have been well acquainted with Peter because it is to her house that he goes after his deliverance from prison (Acts 12:12), apparently as a matter of use and wont. It seems to have been the center of the Christian Church in Jerusalem, and it is widely thought to have been there that the Last

Supper was held. The young man with the pitcher in 14:13 may have been Mark. This might well connect up with that odd little allusion (14:51-52) to the young man in the Garden of Gethsemane who when Jesus was arrested escaped the clutches of the hostile mob by leaving his blanket, which was all he had on, in their hands. This irrelevant detail—omitted by Matthew and Luke—has been compared by Streeter to an item in a press report of a railway accident, where after describing the crash and confusion, the groans of the injured and the agony of the dying, the account continues: "Just then Mr. John Smith lost his pocket handkerchief." What was the point of this vivid interpolation unless the young man was the writer himself and that this is Mark's signature to the gospel? At all events, whatever his connection with our Lord, his connection with Peter is clear. Peter calls him "my son" (I Pet. 5:13), and it is quite possible that John Mark had been converted by him at one of the meetings in his mother's house.

His career then becomes closely interwoven with the missionary journeys of Paul through cousin Barnabas, and St. Luke, the author of Acts, seems to go out of his way to mention him. It is hardly likely that this is because of Mark's importance as a missionary—he is there rather in the capacity of a batman missionary—but it may well be because Luke, the author of the third gospel, is very interested in Mark, the author of the book that he himself had used. Mark then is first brought by Paul and Barnabas from Jerusalem to Antioch (Acts 12:25), and from there he accompanies them on their first missionary journey (13:5). They went to Cyprus—which was Barnabas' native place—and then for some reason when they got to Perga in Pamphylia (13:13), Mark left them and went back to Jerusalem. It may have been that he was homesick, or that he preferred to work with Peter in Jerusalem, or that he was afraid of the perils of the expedition into the wilds of Asia Minor. At all events he was the cause of a split between Paul and Barnabas because when they started out on their second missionary journey, Barnabas wanted to bring Mark, but Paul would not have him (15:38). The result was that Paul and Barnabas separated. Barnabas took Mark to Cyprus while Paul went on with Silas through Syria and Cilicia. There is no more mention of Mark in Acts, but the breach with Paul was apparently healed because he reappears in Rome as a fellow worker and a comfort (Col. 4:10–11, Philem.:24) during Paul's imprisonment. From the passage in Colossians it would seem that Mark intended to go to Asia Minor and that Paul was preparing the Christians at Colossae to make him welcome. Apparently he went there because later Paul writes again from prison, this time to Timothy, telling him to bring Mark to Rome because he was a useful sort of person (2 Tim. 4:11). The last we hear of him in the New Testament suggests that he had returned to Rome and joined not only Paul but Peter, for Peter in a letter from there refers to his being with him (1 Pet. 5:13)—Babylon means Rome here—and we can assume that it is from this time particularly that much of Mark's material in the shape of Peter's firsthand recollections of Jesus' life and teaching is derived. Tradition says that after Peter's martyrdom Mark visited Egypt, founded the church at Alexandria and himself died a martyr's death. Later legend adds that his body was removed from Alexandria to Venice, which was placed under his protection, hence the lion in the standard of the city and the magnificent cathedral of San Marco.

Where, when and why was it written?

Where

Everything points to Rome as the place where Mark's gospel was written. Both the references 2 Tim. 4:11 and 1 Pet. 5:13 and the testimony of Papias, Irenaeus (*c.* 180) and other early authorities confirm it. There are certain indications in the gospel itself that it was written for non-Jewish readers—Aramaic phrases are translated; more than that, Latin technical words are used; and such passages as 7:3–4, 12:42 and 11:13 point to a place of origin where Palestinian customs, coinage and climate are unknown.

When

The date of the gospel can be firmly fixed between A.D. 65 and 70. Irenaeus (A.D. 180) says it was written after the deaths of the apostles Peter and Paul, and Clement of Rome (A.D. 96) says Peter and Paul were martyred in the great persecution under Nero in A.D. 64. Tacitus gives a graphic account of this massacre of the Christians who were made the scapegoats for the mysterious fire that had destroyed more than half of the city and that Nero himself was suspected of starting. Christians were covered with the skins of wild beasts and torn to pieces by dogs, crucified, burned alive or used as human torches to light up the grisly scene of their own destruction. Nero, completely mad, provided his own palace gardens for the entertainment and took part in the chariot races. If the gospel was written after Peter's death, it was likely to have been very soon after, and as there is no reference to the fall of Jerusalem that took place in A.D. 70 (cf. 13:1, etc.), it must be before that date. Within these five years the most probable date is reckoned to be 65-67.

Why

The immediate cause of the writing of the gospel was clearly the death of Peter, the chief eyewitness of the early Church. Mark's desire to combine this firsthand information with the general floating knowledge about Jesus within the framework of the early preaching of the Good News is understandable. The living authority was dead; the next best thing was to preserve what he had taught for the edification of the Christian Church in Rome. There was also the need to strengthen the faith of the little community, which must have been badly shaken by the violence of the persecution. Chapter 13, for example, is probably a contemporary message assuring them that this, though bad enough, is not the end of the world (13:7). The great tribulation (13:19) when the stars will fall (13:25) and antichrist appear (13:14) as a prelude to the Messianic kingdom is not yet—the gospel must be preached to the nations before that happens (13:10). So in a sense, the gospel is also a call addressed to the Church in Rome to return to its missionary task.

Peter's part in the gospel

Mark in making up his gospel had three sources of information. First, there was the common knowledge that was in circulation through the preaching of the missionaries—the outline of Jesus' life, the story of his Passion and Resurrection, incidents, parables and sayings used by Christian teachers in their work; second, his own very probable firsthand experience of the last days at Jerusalem; third, what he had gleaned from St. Peter. If we did not know who the author of the second gospel was, all we could have said was that it was the earliest attempt to collect all the floating oral and written traditions about Jesus that were in circulation in the Church in Rome in A.D. 65. A parallel case would be a man sitting down to write the life of Franklin D. Roosevelt by collecting press cuttings, local gossip from Washington and Hyde Park. He could produce a biography of sorts. But to compile a good biography, he would need either to have been a member of Roosevelt's inner circle or at least to have known one of them well. It is the personal touches that count—the authentic note of the man who can say: I was there. And without a doubt the great authority that Mark's gospel enjoyed was just that he had such a member of the inner circle of Jesus to draw

on. It was Peter's name behind him that ensured
not only that his gospel should be regarded as authoritative in the Church in Rome but also that
Matthew and Luke should later on use it so exten-
sively. If, then, we can see for ourselves traces in
Mark's gospel that indicate that the incidents recorded come from an actual eyewitness, then we
shall feel that we are as close to the life of Jesus
as we shall ever get. Such traces can in fact be
found.

The main characteristic of Mark's gospel is the
vividness and realism of the narrative. But this is
not merely the kind of vividness that comes from
an active imagination. The gospel was written in
Rome, yet it breathes the air of Palestine. This
might, of course, be due to the fact that Mark himself was a Jew, but it can hardly account for the
countless small details in the gospel that point to an
actual spectator of the events described. Notice
how realistically the attitude, expressions and ges-
tures of Jesus are noted; how the comments of the
disciples and the crowd are remembered. A secondhand narrator would say that Jesus blessed the
children who were brought to him, but this gospel
says *He took them in His arms* (10:16). When Jesus
healed the man with the withered hand *He looked
round with anger* (3:5) because the Pharisees were
trying to trap him. When the rich young man came
to him, it is not only the dialogue—the important
part—that is recorded but also that the young man
ran to Jesus and *knelt* before him and that when he
heard what he must do *his face fell* (10:17 ff.).
Surely this is not vivid imagination but actual remi-

niscence of someone who was there. How better can we explain such a story as the healing of the epileptic boy (9:14–29), told here with so much detail that Matthew and Luke have glossed over, other than that it is a clearly remembered experience of one who accompanied Jesus to the scene, who was not afraid to record that the disciples could not heal the boy or that they asked him the reason of their failure afterwards? So also must it have been an eyewitness who saw Jesus during the storm on the lake asleep in the stern of the boat with *His head pillowed on the rowers' cushion* (4:38), who saw him sitting in the women's court of the Temple opposite the alms-boxes watching the people dropping their money into them (12:41), or who with awe in his heart saw that lonely figure striding ahead on the road with his face set towards Jerusalem (10:32). It has been suggested that if in certain passages of the gospel the word "we" is substituted for "they"—as if the person speaking had actually been there—a definite impression of firsthand reporting is given, for example, 9:14, 9:33, 10:32 and 6:30–33 where the fact of having no time even to get a meal would be likely to impress someone who had been there but is unlikely to have been mentioned in a general floating tradition. Compare also 5:5, 6:40, 8:24, 6:56. So in various incidents concerning Peter—in some cases mentioning him by name where the other gospels say "the disciples" or "they"—it is difficult not to feel that this is Peter's own story that we are listening to, for example, the healing of Peter's mother-in-law (1:29–37), the fig tree episode (11:21),

Peter's denial of Jesus (14:66–72) and such passages as 1:36 and 16:7. The same thing is indicated by the fact that Mark preserves the Aramaic that Jesus spoke on occasions where Matthew and Luke give only the Greek translation, for example, 5:41, 7:34, 15:34, and perhaps also by the omission of Jesus' special blessing to Peter that Matthew gives in 16:17–19. It is therefore safe to say that we have the strongest grounds for believing that here in the earliest gospel we have direct access through St. Peter to the life and work of Jesus. The fact that so many of these reminiscences, for example, 8:33, 9:5–6, 10:28, 14:29, 14:37, 14:66–72, are damaging to Peter's reputation may well be connected with his martyrdom—his last stand for his faith had blotted out all his past weaknesses and showed how in Christ even the weakest Christian could be made strong.

Mark's part in the gospel

What, then, was Mark's contribution—merely that of a stenographer? Did he string together these reminiscences of Peter after the apostle's death without any attempt to bring the incidents into a sequence? It is notable that Mark's gospel has a certain staccato effect. The word "straightway" occurs over forty times, and on each occasion it serves to bridge a gap between what may well have been —on the surface at least—incidents separated by long spaces of time. The fact that there is no Sermon on the Mount, indeed very little teaching and few parables, heightens the abruptness with which one event leads on to another. The absence of teaching may well be accounted for by the fact that Q was already known to Mark and that his gospel was designed to supplement it as the "action" part of Jesus' ministry. But it is easy to see how some scholars have come to the conclusion that there is no order in Mark's gospel at all—no chronology—and therefore no hope of ever basing a life of Jesus on the events recorded there. In this view all we have is a haphazard stringing together of anecdotes without reference to when they happened, and joined together crudely by such expressions as "straightway," suggesting that there was a time sequence. As we have seen, however, the character of the earliest Christian preaching was in a sense chronological. The framework of the sermons recorded, for example, in Acts 10:36–43, shows clearly that a historical outline of Jesus' life was in existence from the beginning, with special emphasis on the events in Jerusalem. John Mark as an ordinary church member, not to say teaching missionary, would know this very well so that we should expect to find some real sequence of events in his gospel and not a chance assortment of isolated incidents. And indeed a chronological sequence can be found. If the following passages are grouped together, they will be seen to form a clearly progressive outline of the Galilean ministry: 1:14–15, 21–22, 39; 2:13; 3:7, 13–19; 4:33–34; 6:7, 12, 13, 30.

Based on these passages, we can detect three stages in Jesus' ministry in Galilee: (1) a period when he preached in the various synagogues of the district, (2) a period of open-air preaching to crowds by the lakeside, (3) a period of retreat in the hills with a few disciples who were sent out from there on a teaching and healing mission. The most likely explanation is that this was the chronological framework inherited and taught by Mark in common with all missionaries—the general substance of the tradition concerning Jesus current in Palestine. This outline, then, together no doubt with isolated incidents that were commonly known among the missionaries, would be Mark's contribution to the gospel. Into this he has inserted Peter's reminiscences, and the result is a lack of continuity noticed as early as Papias, which, however, is only apparent. Here, then, in Mark's gospel as we have it are combined two extremely important and reliable sources of knowledge for any study of the life of Jesus: (1) a common tradition giving an outline of Jesus' ministry originating in the country where these events took place and (2) supplementary evidence from one of the inner circle. When we use St. Mark's gospel as a solid foundation for a life of Jesus, we are therefore building on very firm ground indeed.

III

Luke

We found in Mark's gospel two very reliable sources of information about the ministry of Jesus —the reminiscences of Peter and the outline of Jesus' life that was common property in the early days of the Church. In all this, however, there is very little notice taken of what Jesus taught, and Mark apparently wrote his gospel to supplement an already existing collection of the sayings of Jesus. Where is such a collection to be found? The original document Q, which contained this teaching, has been lost, but fortunately most of the contents can be gathered from the works of Matthew and Luke, who have both drawn largely on Mark and Q to form their gospels. Scholars are not altogether agreed on the question of whether Matthew or Luke reproduces Q more accurately; the differences are not fundamental, but the balance seems to come down in favor of Luke.

Can we reconstruct Q?

In some cases the correspondence between Matthew and Luke is very close indeed; in others it is fairly slight, which may be due to the variations in the copies of Q that they themselves used. Ultimately it is impossible to say exactly what was contained in Q; various attempts have been made to reproduce the original, and probably the following passages would roughly be agreed on by most scholars as constituting Q though not exhausting it: Luke 3:7–9, 16–17; 4:1–13; 6:20–49; 7:1–10, 18–35; 9:57–62; 10:2–3, 8–16, 21–24; 11:9–52; 12:1–12, 22–59; 13:18–30, 34–35; 14:15–27; 16:13, 16–18; 17:1–6, 22–37; 19:11–27. Q is very important. It contains very little narrative, but because of its early date, we may take it that its account of the teaching of Jesus is as authentic as anything we can hope to get. On the other hand, there is no reason to despise other collections of sayings of Jesus that occur in Mark, Matthew or Luke or to imagine that Q contained all that Jesus ever said. Many a saying of his must have failed to find a place in this collection either because it was not understood or did not make a sufficient impression.

Who was the author?

All the early Church commentators are agreed that the third gospel was written by Luke, the companion of St. Paul's missionary expeditions. From the prologue style and internal evidence of the book of Acts, it is clear that it was written by the same author so that the third gospel is the first volume of a two-volume work dealing with the life of Jesus and the beginnings of Christianity. Both books are dedicated to Theophilus, probably a

Roman official, and it would seem from the high literary quality of the gospel and the pains that the author has taken to produce a systematic and orderly document that it was intended for a wider public than the Christian community. It is in fact a Christian apologia to the pagan world: an attempt to show that the gospel, far from being an affair of a small Jewish sect, is universal in its appeal, and that it is not a disruptive but an integrating factor in society. Luke is mentioned in three letters of Paul—Col. 4:14, where he is called "the beloved physician"; 2 Tim. 4:11; and Philemon 24, where Paul calls him a fellow worker. Tradition always asserts that Luke was not a Jew. Eusebius goes further and says he was a Syrian from Antioch, and certainly the Book of Acts is well informed about what took place there. Luke may have been one of the earliest Gentile converts admitted by Paul, but there is no certainty about his association with Paul until the appearance of the first-person plural in the narrative in Acts 16:10. We may infer from this that Luke joined Paul at Troas and crossed from there to Macedonia, thereby becoming one of the first evangelists of Europe. Perhaps the presence of a doctor in the missionary team was necessary to cope with Paul's attacks of what he calls his "thorn in the flesh." At all events when Paul and Silas left Philippi (Acts 17:1), Luke seems to have stayed behind —note that "we" is replaced by "they"—to supervise the young Macedonian church there. This kept him busy for several years, for when Paul calls there (Acts 20:5–6) on his way to Jerusalem, we find Luke ready to accompany him and the other

delegates who were making this visit to the mother
Church with gifts for the poor of the community
from the members of the Gentile churches. There,
as we know, Paul was arrested and sent to Caesarea,
where he was imprisoned for two years, A.D. 56–58
or 57–59. During all this time, Luke was with him
but at liberty—a highly important fact. Caesarea
itself was a center of Christian activity directed by
Philip, the apostle to the Samaritans; it was within
easy reach of Galilee and Judaea; and there were
countless opportunities in this period for Luke to
gather together, both from eyewitnesses and hear-
say, information about the life and times of Jesus,
which afterward he incorporated in his gospel.
From Caesarea, Luke went with Paul to Rome—
from his pen we get that vivid picture of the ship-
wreck at Malta—and presumably he was with the
apostle until his death. Luke's own end is unknown:
tradition says he died in Greece and that his body
was removed by the Emperor Constantine to the
Church of the Apostles in Constantinople.

He is also said to have been a painter—largely on
the strength of a painting now in S. Maria Maggiore
at Rome, which was found in the catacombs. It is
a picture of the Virgin with the inscription "one of
seven painted by Lukas." Whatever truth there is in
that identification, there is no doubt about Luke's
literary accomplishments. He was a master of good
Greek style—the most polished writer among the
evangelists, and the most careful and scholarly historian. He appears to have been a shrewd observer
of both men and matters and was certainly a faithful
friend. There are some traces of his interest in med-

ical affairs, the most intriguing being in his adaptation of the Markan story of the woman with the issue of blood. Mark (5:25 ff.), in his usual downright way, says she had spent all she had and suffered a lot at the hands of the doctors and instead of getting better grew steadily worse. You can see Dr. Luke pursing his lips as he comes to this bit of Mark's gospel. He does not mind admitting that she had spent all her money on physicians and that they could not cure her, but to say that she had suffered a lot from their bad diagnoses and that instead of getting better she grew worse was going too far, and so he leaves that bit out (8:43 ff.). It has been noticed, too, that Luke's knowledge of nautical matters (cf. Acts 27) is accurate but unprofessional, and it has been suggested that he may have been a ship's doctor. Another suggestion is that he may have been a freed slave. Doctors were commonly slaves in those days, the -*as* ending of Lukas was frequent in slave names, and possibly Theophilus may have been his master. All this, however, is largely speculation.

How did Luke construct his gospel?

In the prologue to his gospel (1:1–4) Luke, addressing Theophilus, states that "forasmuch as many have taken in hand to draw up a narrative concerning those matters which have been fulfilled among us, even as they delivered them unto us which from the beginning were eyewitnesses and ministers of the word, it seemed good to me also, having traced the course of all things accurately from the first to write unto thee in order." Here, then, is the careful scholar and historian, acknowledging his authorities almost in the classical manner. From a study of Luke's gospel, it is clear that at least two written sources lay to his hand—one, Mark, and the other, Q. More than half of Mark's gospel has been incorporated in Luke, and between 200 and 250 verses that Luke has in common with Matthew can safely be attributed to Q. But in addition to this material, there is the matter peculiar to Luke that makes up about half his gospel and falls into two sections: various narratives—for example, Martha and Mary, Zacchaeus, parables such as the good Samaritan and the prodigal son and odd sayings (mostly in chaps. 9:51–18:14), and—the birth stories (chaps. 1–2). It has been suggested that the method Luke adopted was first to make a first sketch of his gospel (Proto Luke) by combining Q with the special material that is peculiar to his gospel, which he probably gathered at Caesarea during Paul's imprisonment and may well have written down there or soon after. If this theory is correct, it means that in this gospel we have another very early and reliable source independent of Mark dating from about A.D. 60. This first draft, consisting of selections from Q and L (Luke's special sources of information), will then have been combined with selections from Mark about twenty years later. Probably at the same time, the Nativity stories, possibly in Aramaic, were added to give us the gospel as we now have it. This final stage probably took place between 75 and 85.

Characteristics of Luke's gospel

We have noticed already the different methods of approach adopted by Mark and Luke to the task of writing a gospel. It is only to be expected, therefore, that the first notable characteristic of the third gospel is its *literary merit.* If we think of the incidents and parables in the gospels as a whole that come most readily to our minds, it will surprise us to find how many of them occur in Luke. Parables already mentioned like the prodigal son (15:11 ff.) and the good Samaritan (10:30 ff.); others like the rich man and Lazarus (16:19 ff.) and the Pharisee and publican (18:9 ff.); pen pictures like the scene between Martha and Mary (10:38 ff.) or the walk to Emmaus (24:13 ff.); or character studies like that of Zaccheus (19:1 ff.), the Roman centurion (7:2 ff.), the father and elder brother in the story of the prodigal (15:11 ff.)—all of these are superbly done with the deft touch of a master hand. Little wonder that Renan called this "the most beautiful book in the world."

Another feature of Luke's gospel that is very striking is its *universal* outlook. It is above all things the gospel for the Gentiles. All the crazy shibboleths of Judaism disappear, and Christ appears as the Savior not of the Jews but of mankind. The first barrier is broken down when Jesus on his way to the Cross makes no distinction between Jews and Samaritans and is prepared to lodge in one of their villages (9:52). The age-old feud is made to look ridiculous when Jesus draws his immortal picture of the man who has since become a byword for all good works—the good Samaritan (10:30)—and when he heals the ten lepers, Luke records that the only one to come back to return thanks was one of the hated apostates (17:11 ff.). But greater than the bridge between local rivalries is the one that the gospel throws between Jews and Gentiles. From the very beginning of the gospel, the universal note is struck—peace on earth, goodwill towards men (2:14). The Christ who comes is to be the light who will enlighten the Gentiles (2:29–32). So throughout the gospel there is this emphasis on the wideness of the Good News—the conditions of entrance to the kingdom are not national privilege. Many Jews may be left outside while Gentiles from the four corners of the earth stream in (13:29). A Roman soldier is praised for having greater faith than Jesus had found in all Israel (7:9). So the keynote of the gospel is struck in the command (24:47) to go out and preach the gospel unto all the nations, and in keeping with this idea, Jesus' descent is not considered to begin with Abraham the Father of the Jews but with Adam the father of humanity (3:38).

Another notable characteristic is Luke's interest in *social questions*. He does not condemn wealth out of hand. Zacchaeus (19:1 ff.) is a rich man who is kindly treated by Jesus, and women of means look after him (8:3). But Luke's sympathies are all with the poor. This is clear as early in the gospel as the Magnificat (1:46), that "revolutionary" document that approves of princes being cast down from their thrones and men of low degree being exalted, of the hungry being filled and the rich being sent away empty. Jesus quotes as his mission at Nazareth the prophecy that says: "The spirit of the Lord is upon me because he anointed me to preach good tidings to the poor" (4:18). In Matthew where the Beatitude says "Blessed are the poor in spirit" (5:3), Luke simply says "Blessed are the poor" (6:20) and adds the warning peculiar to his gospel: "Woe unto you that are rich" (6:24). Jesus denounces the Pharisees as "lovers of money" (16:14) and calls wealth "the mammon of unrighteousness" (16:9). Many of the parables peculiar to Luke deal with finance in one way or another—the two debtors (7:41 ff.), the rich fool (12:16 ff.), the tower builder (14:28 ff.), the unjust steward (16:1 ff.), the rich man and Lazarus (16:19 ff.).

More important, perhaps, is the fact that the Jesus of Luke's gospel is preeminently the *friend of the poor, the outcast, and the black sheep of society.* He consorts with publicans and sinners to the indignation of the orthodox. St. Luke is indeed as Dante describes him the "scribe of the gentleness of Christ." It is the poor, the maimed, the lame and the blind who should be at the table of the real disciple of Christ (14:13), and it is they who are the guests at the great supper in the parable (14:16 ff.). So it is with the city prostitute (7:36 ff.), the penitent thief (23:39 ff.), the little quisling (19:1 ff.), all in real life or with the fictitious figures of the wayward son (15:11 ff.) and the humble publican in the temple (18:13). The Jesus of these incidents and tales is no sentimentalist. Luke does not give us a gospel that is easy. The conditions of discipleship are strict and uncompromising. If anything, he shows us the sterner side of Jesus. Where Matthew says, "He that loveth father or mother more than me is not worthy of me" (10:37), Luke's version reads, "If any man cometh unto me and hateth not his own father and mother . . . he cannot be my disciple" (14:26). Further examples of this can be found in 14:33-34 and 9:57-62. The Jesus of Luke's gospel who so remarkably strikes us as the great-hearted friend of the outcast is also the Jesus who tells his disciples, "Even . . . when ye shall have done all the things that are commanded you, say, We are unprofitable servants: we have done that which it was our duty to do" (17:10). This mingling of the compassion and the severity of Christ is one of the most valuable angles the third gospel gives us on Jesus' nature.

Everyone notices that Luke's gospel gives most prominence to *women*. Apart from the birth stories where we read of Mary, Elizabeth and Anna, Luke alone introduces Joanna and Susanna (8:3), the widow of Nain (7:11 ff.), the prostitute (7:36 ff.), the women of Jerusalem who followed Jesus to the Cross (23:27) and the parables of the woman with the lost coin (15:8 ff.) and the importunate widow (18:1 ff.). In this connection it is worth noticing how Luke enjoys picturing domestic scenes—the Pharisee's dinner table (7:36 ff.), the house of Martha and Mary (10:38 ff.), the house at Emmaus (24:30) or, in the stories, the vivid picture of the woman sweeping out her room (15:8), the prodigal's father making arrangements for his homecoming (15:22 ff.), the man in bed with his children (11:7).

In this gospel there is more reference to *prayer* than in the other Synoptics, and this fact is worth noting, particularly because Luke's references occur in narratives that are not peculiar to his book. Jesus prays at his baptism (3:21), he prays before selecting the twelve disciples (6:12), he prays before the Transfiguration (9:28); the Lord's Prayer is given in response to the disciples' request, "Lord teach us to pray," when they had seen Jesus himself in prayer (11:1). He prays for Peter (22:32), for himself (22:41) and for his enemies (23:34). The two words from the Cross—"Father forgive them" (23:34) and "Father, into thy hands I commend my spirit" (23:46)—are found only in Luke. In the parables of the importunate friend and the importunate widow (18:1 ff.), Jesus teaches the value of persistent prayer, and the story of the Pharisee and the publican (18:9 ff.) shows us the right and the wrong attitude in praying.

Lastly through the whole gospel there rings a note of triumph. Here we find these great hymns of praise—the Magnificat, the Benedictus, the Nunc Dimittis, the Gloria in Excelsis (chaps. 1 and 2). From the angelic voice that the shepherds heard, "Behold I bring you good tidings of great joy" (2:10), to the final picture of the disciples praising God in the Temple (24:53), as Harnack says, "a trumpet note of joy, courage and triumph sounds through the whole Lukan history from the first to the last page." It is the gospel of the youthfulness of Jesus—it tells us most of what we know about his birth and all we know about his boyhood. Its emphasis is greatly on the social side of his nature—the Jesus in Luke is the friend of humanity, the welcome guest at everyman's table rather than the Man of Sorrows. It is as if Luke is determined to "lift the veil that hides from churlish and gloomy souls the joy which is in the presence of the angels of God" (Adeney).

IV

John

There is no more hotly disputed question in New Testament criticism than the authorship and reliability of the fourth gospel. None of the critics doubts its religious value—all would agree that as devotional literature there is no greater book in the Bible and no author who has a deeper insight into the unique relationship between the Christian and his Master. What is disputed is how much reliance we can place on the incidents recorded in the gospel and the words spoken by Jesus as being an authentic account of what actually happened and what he actually said. Why should this question arise at all? The answer is clear, for even on the most superficial reading of the four gospels it is obvious that they divide themselves naturally into two types—the first three, Matthew, Mark, and Luke on the one hand, called because of their resemblance to one another "synoptic," and the fourth gospel on the other hand constituting a type of its own. Why do we divide the gospels so readily into these two groups, and what does the difference between them consist of?

Differences between the Synoptics and John

The first obvious difference is that in the Synoptic gospels most of Jesus' ministry takes place in Galilee, with the only one visit to Jerusalem in the last week of his life, whereas in John's gospel, Jesus moves back and forth between Galilee and Jerusalem, but his chief activity is in Jerusalem.

Secondly, it would appear from the Synoptic gospels that Jesus' ministry lasted only approximately one year, while John mentions three different Passovers, implying a ministry certainly of over two years (2:13, 6:4, 11:55).

Thirdly, according to the first three gospels, the Last Supper was the ordinary Jewish Passover, while John would make it a special pre-Passover meal, Christ himself being crucified as the Jews were killing the Paschal lambs.

Other details of variations in the narratives occur. Jesus calls the disciples from fishing in the Sea of Galilee (in the Synoptics) but from following the Baptist to join him at the Jordan (in the fourth gospel). So also the cleansing of the Temple in one case comes at the end of Jesus' ministry and in the other at the beginning.

Particularly is the difference felt in the matter of Jesus' teaching. In the Synoptics Jesus' utterances are short and pithy, proverbs and parables of a simple kind. In John these short sayings become long discourses, sometimes involved and subtle. Where Jesus in the Synoptics teaches mostly about the Kingdom and conditions of entrance and life in it, in John he speaks mostly of himself and his relationship to God.

There is, too, a difference in the general picture
that the fourth gospel gives of Jesus. In the Synoptics—especially Mark and Luke—there is no attempt to emphasize the divine nature of Jesus at the
expense of his humanity. Matthew, as we have
seen, is inclined to alter Mark in the direction of
suppressing the more human side of Jesus' nature.
But John seems to go even further. Jesus is not
baptized at the Jordan, he is not tempted, he does
not need to pray for strength, he utters no cry of
dereliction on the Cross. In other words, the things
that would make Jesus man are left out. Now the
first question to ask ourselves is: Are these differences irreconcilable? If they are, then of course one
or other must be wrong. Either the Synoptics or
John must give the true account. They cannot both
be right, and as Mark is the oldest gospel the infer-
ence is that John is unreliable. But is this not a false
dilemma? Let us look at the points of difference in
detail.

It is true that in the Synoptic gospels a full account is given of the Galilean ministry, and Jerusalem is only reached in Passion week. But it is only
in Passion week that any attempt is made to give a
chronological account of Jesus' movements; the
rest of his ministry is rather sketched in broad outline with certain incidents inserted. There is no
evidence in the Synoptics that contradicts the importance John gives to a Jerusalem ministry as well
as a Galilean. It is much more likely indeed that
Jesus visited Jerusalem oftener than the Synoptics
suggest. How else can we explain his cry over the
city: "O Jerusalem Jerusalem . . . how often would
I have gathered thy children together even as a hen

gathereth her chickens under her wings and ye would not?" (Matt. 23:37, Luke 13:34—a saying from Q.) In other words this is not two conflicting pictures but two complementary pictures.

As to the length of Jesus' ministry, the Synoptic gospels merely suggest that it lasted a year or over, they nowhere say so. (John's two or three years would harmonize with the following facts: Jesus was born, as Matthew says, while Herod was king. Herod died in 4 B.C. Luke further tells us that Jesus was about thirty when he began to preach, and tradition says he was crucified in A.D. 29.) We must remember too that in this and other differences it is not a question of three against one but of one against one. The real issue is between Mark and John.

On the variation in the day on which the Last Supper was held, it is much more likely that John's version is the correct one. Jesus suggests in Luke 22:15 that he had wanted to celebrate the Passover with his disciples, implying that his wish had not been granted. Further, it is not easy to see how if the Passover was in progress such secular affairs as the arrest, trial and crucifixion of a malefactor could be carried out. It now appears that there were two separate days on which the Passover was celebrated: one, the official date, and two, an alternative day favored by nonconformist religious groups such as the Qumran community, which produced the Dead Sea Scrolls. Jesus and his disciples could have formed a similar group.

Regarding details that appear to conflict, like the calling of the disciples and the cleansing of the temple, is it impossible that they may have taken place on different occasions? There may well have been two calls and two cleansings.

Now look at Jesus' teaching. In the Synoptic gospels when Jesus uses his short proverbial style of utterance or his parables, he is talking mostly to the crowds. In John's gospel he is mainly talking to the inner circle of disciples or engaged in controversy with the Jewish religious leaders. In the one case his words have to be simple and clearly intelligible and easily remembered; in the other the type of discourse is perfectly in harmony with the purpose. As for the objection that in the fourth gospel Jesus talks mainly about himself and his sonship while the Jesus of the Synoptics does not, the whole question depends upon what attitude we take toward Jesus. If we approach the gospels determined to find him a good man, a great teacher, a heroic martyr, we shall no doubt discredit all he says about himself in John as unhistorical. We should also, however, have to discredit such a saying as "All things are delivered unto me of my Father and no man knoweth the Son but the Father, neither knoweth any man the Father save the Son and he to whomsoever the Son will reveal him." This saying does not occur in John but in the ancient and trustworthy document Q (Matt. 11:27, Luke 10:22). If, on the other hand, we are prepared to admit that Jesus may have been what he claimed to be and was not an arrogant lunatic—for there is no alternative—then what he says in John's gospel about himself is precisely what we should expect.

This attempt to prove the author's deliberate intention to conceal the human side of Jesus is not convincing. Other features of the Synoptic story that emphasize his divinity are likewise omitted, for example, the Last Supper and the Transfiguration, while clear indications of his humanity are included, for example, 4:6.

The first point to be established is, then, that the differences between the Synoptic gospels and John are more apparent than real. The question whether John is right or whether the Synoptics are right is to be answered on the whole by the statement that both are right. By and large what we have are two complementary accounts. Without John, the Synoptics are incomplete; without the Synoptics, John is one-sided. That is not to say that on small matters one or other may appear to have preserved the more accurate account, but the fact to remember is that the more accurate account is as likely to be found in John as in the other three.

Who was the author?

The second point that has to be settled is: Who was the author? For not only has it been used as an argument against the reliability of the fourth gospel that it does not square with the Synoptics, but it has also been widely held that far from being written by John the Apostle, this gospel was the work of some unknown though inspired Christian with a gift of imagination writing at the beginning of the second century A.D. It is quite clear how important this question is. It goes right to the heart of the problem of the reliability of the gospel as a whole.

If the fourth gospel differs in tone and detail from the other three, and it is proved that the author has no more direct knowledge of Jesus than anyone else with a copy of Mark's gospel in his hands and a vivid creative imagination, then no matter how fine a devotional work he produces, it is of no more historical value than Thomas à Kempis' *Imitation of Christ* or *Pilgrim's Progress* or any other work of the kind. If however, the author is one of the apostolic circle or closely connected with it, we have not merely the product of pious meditation on the life of Jesus but a record of deeds that were actually done and words that were actually spoken.

In the gospel itself (21:20–24), the author is described as "the disciple whom Jesus loved." Who was this Beloved Disciple? As far back as the second century, tradition is unanimous that he was John the son of Zebedee, not only one of the twelve but one of the inmost circle. Tradition also adds that he lived to a very old age at Ephesus, and this would fit in with the statement in 21:23. Despite this, many scholars insist on producing reasons why John the son of Zebedee could not have been the Beloved Disciple: he was too fiery and impulsive, he was one of the Sons of Thunder, he wanted to call down fire from heaven on the Samaritans, he disputed for a place of honor in the kingdom. But is this any reason why Jesus should not have loved him? Is it not sentimentality born of traditional pictures of a rather effeminate disciple leaning on the Lord's bosom that sees anything incongruous in the Son of Thunder being the Beloved Disciple? Such alternatives to identifying

John the Apostle with the disciple whom Jesus loved as to invent a wholly imaginary young man who is supposed to be the "ideal disciple," or an anonymous youth who may have been the other disciple who ran with Peter to the tomb (20:3–8) and is to be identified wholly conjecturally with other anonymous characters who appear in the gospel narratives (Mk. 11:5–6, 14:13–14, John 18: 15–16), or Lazarus, or the Rich Young Ruler, seem to be wholly unnecessary and sheer speculation.

What is, however, a valid argument against John the son of Zebedee having written the gospel with his own hand is the fact that the Epistles of John later on in the New Testament are clearly, from the point of view of style and contents, by the same hand as the fourth gospel, and the writer of the second and third epistles of John calls himself "the Elder" who, tradition says, was also at Ephesus. The easiest solution is, then, to think of John the Elder as the actual writer of the gospel but getting his material from John the son of Zebedee, the Beloved Disciple, much in the same way as Mark wrote his gospel from the reminiscences of Peter. (This would explain the fact that the writer of the fourth gospel uses Mark and Luke as sources; cf. John 6:7; Mk. 6:37; Jn. 12:3–4; Mk. 14:3,5; John 12:2; Luke 10:38. He would not have done this if he had been the apostle, but he corrects them with the confidence of one who has authoritative knowledge apart from them.) This would explain the fact that there is displayed in the gospel an intimate knowledge of Jewish matters and countryside— which would come from John the Apostle—side by side with a more philosophic strain, which would hardly come from a Galilean fisherman but might well come from John the Elder. The date of the gospel is generally agreed to be about the end of the first century: 90–100. Many scholars have more recently argued for an earlier date.

Purpose of the gospel

The third point of importance is to see what were the aims of the author of the fourth gospel. If he had some special purpose in view, it might perhaps account for the difference in tone and substance from the Synoptics. Mark wrote his gospel partly because there was no gospel then in existence, partly to encourage the persecuted Church in Rome. Luke wrote through Theophilus to put the claims of Christianity before the educated Roman world. Matthew wrote to show his Jewish countrymen that here in Jesus the Messiah had come. John states his purpose clearly (20:31): "These are written that you may believe that Jesus is the Christ the Son of God, and that believing you may have life in His name." These words have been misinterpreted so as to cast doubts on the authenticity of the gospel. It has been argued that because John sets out with this doctrinal purpose, this avowed aim of proving that Christ is the Son of God, therefore he must have twisted and perverted the Synoptic record of facts to suit his theological ends. Now it is one thing to say that the fourth evangelist selects certain aspects of Jesus' nature and certain incidents in his ministry to illustrate his thesis; it is quite another thing to say that these incidents, because they serve his purpose, are unhistorical. It makes nonsense of both the gospel and its purpose if we imagine the author sitting down and inventing illustrations of Jesus' Sonship of God that he knows to be untrue. What he may do is to interpret the significance of an event that has taken place, but he must be certain that it *has* taken place; otherwise it has no significance.

Similarly with the teaching of Jesus. When we ask what did Jesus say, do we mean what were literally the sounds he uttered—in other words, a gramophone record, which to us would convey nothing—or do we want rather to know what did Jesus mean, what was the significance of what he said, its universal quality? This is rather what St. John gives us. (William Temple makes a good distinction between the Synoptic and Johannine picture of Jesus as the difference between a photograph and a portrait.) All the gospels—Synoptics included—give us history plus interpretation. And indeed the bare facts of anything that happened in the past are of little value without the interpretative additions of witnesses or recorders. In the fourth gospel what we have more than in the other gospels is the result of meditation and reflection on what Jesus did and said, meditation and reflection on the part of the Beloved Disciple, mellowed by the passing of the years and transmitted through his mind and that of John the Elder onto the pages of the New Testament. The fourth gospel, then, is the work of an artist rather than a scientific historian, but it is in that respect perhaps a truer picture of the life and times of Jesus, just as a good portrait does not catch merely the passing expression of a moment as does a photograph, but gathers the essence of the subject into one likeness.

There is no such thing as a Jesus of history as opposed to a Christ of faith—every word that is written about him in the New Testament or outside of it is a record of the impact he has made upon men. If we say that the Synoptic gospels record more nearly the local setting of these words and incidents in Jesus' life, we must at the same time say that to understand what Jesus means we must set the fourth gospel alongside the Synoptics. John's purpose, then, is to speak from faith to faith—to communicate to his readers what over the years Christ had come to mean to him—and we cannot get closer to the Jesus who walked and talked in Galilee and Judaea than by seeing him through the eyes of the disciple who leant on his bosom. So when Jesus says "I am the Bread of Life," or the "Good Shepherd," or the "Light of the World," we not only can be sure that he said it, but also that the Beloved Disciple had experienced it to be true. This was plain to the early Church as far back as Clement of Alexandria, who wrote, "Having observed that the bodily things had been exhibited in the other gospels John, inspired by the Spirit, produced a spiritual gospel." John's gospel is the life of the historical Jesus seen *sub specie aeternitatis.* He wants to make it clear to the later generations living far away from Palestine that the Good News was not time- or place-conditioned but that men and women of Ephesus who had never seen Palestine and cared nothing for Jewry, who lived in a different kind of world in a different generation, could still become Christ's disciples and share the abundant life. What made Christianity a world religion as much as anything was the fourth gospel's presentation of what was best in Jewish thought in a form that was intellectually acceptable to the wider world.

Contents of the gospel

The fourth gospel is undoubtedly the most rewarding and fruitful book in the New Testament. When we read the Synoptics, we see Jesus as he walked and talked in Galilee and Jerusalem; when we read the letters of Paul, we see there the Christ of faith and experience. The two are not contradictory, but the emphasis lies on different aspects. The fourth gospel shows us how the two are one, how the Jesus who moves in the family circle of Martha and Mary, who talks to men and women on their own level and meets their own peculiar problems, is at the same time God himself in human form. This is a gospel that must be read and read again, and we can read it in the assurance that we have before us no pious work of inspired imagination but an authentic record based on what Jesus did and said. A profitable way to read the gospel is to see it as Jesus' developing revelation of himself. First there is a prologue, 1:1–18. Then, to begin with, Jesus reveals himself to individuals—to the Baptist, to Nathanael, to the disciples at Cana, to Nicodemus, to the woman of Samaria, and to a nobleman

(1:19–4:54). Then in the next three chapters he reveals himself as the giver of a new Law, as a leader, and as a feeder of the multitudes (5–7). Next he shows himself to be the Light of the World, the Good Shepherd, the Son of God (8: 12–10:42). Then he declares himself to be the Resurrection and the Life (11). All this time opposition has progressively increased, and now it has come to a conspiracy to have him killed (12). The prelude to the end is his most intimate and moving revelation of himself to the disciples in the great discourses (13–17), followed by his trial, death and resurrection (18–20). An epilogue completes the gospel (21).

Perhaps some notes on the reading of the gospel might be helpful.

The prologue

What does John mean by the "Word"? Controversy has raged round this question. Some have sought to show that use of the original Greek word *logos* meant that John was simply introducing Greek philosophical speculation into Christian thought. The Stoics used the term "logos" to mean the indwelling reason that fills the universe and links it up with God. Others have said that it is a purely Jewish idea developed from the Wisdom literature of the Old Testament where Wisdom had an almost independent existence as the principle underlying the universe. The answer is probably that John is thinking of both the Greek and the Jewish ideas. But it is not necessary to do more than take it as it stands. The Word of God is God speaking in a way men can understand. What St. John says is that Creation is an uttered thought of God—the expression of God's mind. We are reminded at once of the first chapter of Genesis: "God said: Let there be light." God spoke and it was done—his word created—and we understand Creation as God's work. So God spoke—through the prophets and saints of Israel above all but also in other ways and in other places. But this was not enough. So in the fullness of time the Word became flesh (1:14)—God spoke in a way that everyone could understand, in the human life of Jesus of Nazareth.

Narratives peculiar to John

Apart from teaching material, the stories John gives us that are not found anywhere else are among the best known in the gospels: the visit of Nicodemus to Jesus by night, the Woman at the Well, the Raising of Lazarus, the Washing of the Disciples' Feet, and his Resurrection appearances to Mary Magdalene and Doubting Thomas. The famous and beautiful story of Jesus and the Woman taken in Adultery—a story that has every ring of genuineness (7:53–8:11)—is not found in the oldest manuscript. It is an example of how independent stories existed and were in circulation, some of them becoming incorporated in the gospels and some of them being lost. This one is sometimes found in manuscripts of Luke's gospel after chapter 21.

The discourses

Chapters 14–17, Jesus' words to the disciples before his Passion and the prayer that follows, are perhaps the greatest chapters in the New Testament. Origen said, "The Gospels are the first fruits of all the Scriptures but of the Gospels that of John is the first fruits. No one can apprehend the meaning of it except he have lain on Jesus' breast and received from him Mary to be his mother also." This is particularly true of the meaning of these chapters. The deeper our own experience of the presence of Jesus with us, the more we cherish these words, and there is no surer way of deepening our knowledge of him further than by turning to them again and again. Some have complained that in this gospel it is difficult to know sometimes whether the evangelist or Jesus is speaking, for example, in the story of Nicodemus, chapter 3, where probably at verse 16 the gospel writer continues where Jesus leaves off without any noticeable change of tone. It has been said, therefore, that when we read the words of Jesus in the fourth gospel, we read them at secondhand—it is not Jesus who speaks but the evangelist, and his ways of thought color all that Jesus says. But it is surely just as probable that the process is reversed—old John the son of Zebedee has by dint of a lifetime's reflection on the Master's words molded his own thought forms on his—and what we have is more the mind of Jesus coloring the evangelist's contribution than vice versa.

Symbolism

One of the most far-reaching contributions of this fourth gospel is a feature that is peculiarly its own, and it is a feature that shows just how important this gospel is for a true appreciation of Jesus' work. When Mark tells the stories of the feeding of the multitude, he suggests each time that there was something mysterious about it (6:52 and 8:17–21). Similarly, at the Last Supper Jesus distributes bread to the disciples with the strange words "this is my body" (14:22). When John comes to tell the story of the feeding of the crowd (chap. 6), he connects it up at once with a discourse of Jesus on the "Bread of Life." The bread that Jesus had given to the crowd was a symbol of the spiritual nourishment he had come to give. This is what the Christian Church repeats in its chief sacrament. So with all that Jesus does in the fourth gospel, which is of course but a selection of what the Synoptics tell us, the incident is not told for the sake of telling but as a symbol of some spiritual truth. When Jesus heals a paralytic, it is symbolic of how he heals paralyzed souls; when he makes a blind man see, it is a symbol of how he opens the eyes of the spiritually blind; when he raises Lazarus from the dead, it is a proclamation that Jesus is the Resurrection and the Life, that those who are dead in spirit can be raised in him to eternal life.

BOOK 3
_____

Bible, Church and World

I

The New Israel

For the continuation of the gospel story, we turn to St. Luke's second volume, the Book of Acts. In the latter half of this book, the writer is drawing upon his own knowledge. He himself was one of the missionaries who accompanied Paul on his journeys, and where he was not present himself, he was in an excellent position to know what happened. In the first half of the book, Luke is dependent upon traditions of the various communities referred to and upon those with whom he came in contact who had been involved in these events.

Some of the incidents recorded have obviously grown in the telling, the miraculous element has been heightened and the chronology is not always certain. On his own showing, though, Luke is a careful scholar as well as a skillful author. He has to trace, in twenty-eight short chapters, the story of the first thirty years of the Church's existence, to show how the movement that began against a purely Jewish background and in totally Jewish thought forms became in that short period a Gentile faith and, from the very heart of the Roman Empire, prepared to win the world for Christ.

This he does in a series of deft sketches in which the growth of the faith, its problems and setbacks, are seen against a colorful panorama of personalities, with all the variety and confusion of Hellenistic civilization. Where we are able to cross-check Luke's accuracy as a historian by archaeological evidence, he emerges with high credit, and we may take the Book of Acts as a substantially reliable reflection of the life and thought of the first generation of Christianity.

The days that followed the Resurrection were for the eleven disciples of Jesus a period of deepening understanding and growing conviction. It is not surprising that what began as doubt and incredulity ended as exhilarating and triumphant certainty. As one after another became certain that the Master was not dead but alive and in their midst, much that he had said about his death and the future became clear. They knew now what he had meant by these cryptic utterances about the necessity for the Son of Man to suffer in order that the Kingdom might come "with power."

They felt within themselves that that new power had come among them. They were no longer the conscience- and terror-stricken fugitives of Good Friday but men afire with a new confidence that, despite all that evil could do, God's Messiah had defeated evil once and for all. It might be that the power of Satan was still around them, but his throne was tottering. In the mighty act of raising Jesus from the dead, God had proven to the world that the reins were not in the hands of the Prince of Darkness but of the King of Kings.

The account of the Ascension presents difficulties only if we treat it as literal description. Like the narrative of the Day of Pentecost, which follows shortly after, it is a pictorial representation of an event that is essentially incapable of prosaic description. In the weeks following the Resurrection, the first stage of the enlightenment of the disciples was accomplished. For this it was necessary that the Risen Christ should himself appear, just as it was necessary at a later stage in the case of St. Paul. When the post-Resurrection appearances ceased, however, giving place to a new development in the situation, there was no other way open to first-century writers of expressing the conviction that the Messiah was now with God than by such a localized description. When they said that he had ascended into heaven, they were simply stating their conviction that the Christ, having triumphed over death, still lived in the perfect relationship to God that he had always enjoyed but was now freed from the limitations of time and space that the Palestinian ministry had imposed upon him.

Before Pentecost, however, there was an important step to be taken. The place of Judas must be filled. And although the man who was chosen is never heard of again, we should note that it was felt that the number of the Twelve should be maintained, and that eligibility for inclusion in the inner circle depended on the candidate's having been present throughout the historical ministry of Jesus and therefore being able to speak from firsthand knowledge. This insistence from the very beginning of the Church's existence on historical evidence is significant and revealing (Acts 1:15 ff.).

The day of Pentecost, or Whitsunday, marked a further stage. This was the Jewish festival that took place fifty days after Passover. It was marked by offering the first fruits of the harvest to God and had become associated with the giving of the Law to Moses. Now, fifty days after the New Exodus, it becomes the occasion of a collective religious experience that is the beginning of the Christian mission to the world. Indeed, it is the birthday of the Christian Church. This growing sense of certainty and jubilation, this sense of living in a new dimension, of being lifted above the world and its problems, which had been transforming the disciples since the day of the Resurrection, now communicated itself to the whole gathering of those who had been persuaded that Christ had risen.

They were caught up in an overpowering experience that they could only afterward describe in terms of rushing wind and tongues of fire. With these conventional Old Testament symbols of the presence of God, they sought to convey what was uppermost in their minds, that what had happened was supernatural, that the Spirit of God had swept across them, and that this was the climax to the miracle of the Resurrection. The power of Jesus had not ended on the Cross, nor by the Ascension had it been transferred to another sphere; it was here in their midst, living, uplifting, exhilarating. They were new men indeed. This was the life of the Kingdom that Christ had promised.

In the narrative of Acts (2:1–13), two elements are intertwined. The first is that as a result of this communal experience, the group became ecstatic, as the early prophets had also been when the Spirit of God seized upon them, and as has been the case at many religious revivals since that day. It was the physical counterpart of an overpowering inward experience. To the bystanders, they were behaving like drunk men (2:13). Luke has, however, introduced a second element, which is not original, when he identifies this ecstatic condition, which in the Authorized Version is called "speaking with tongues," with the power to speak each other's language, so that each man in this crowd drawn from all parts of the civilized world was able to understand his neighbor. This in fact could have been accomplished merely by using Aramaic and Greek, one of which would have been understood by all present.

Luke's point is rather to suggest that as a result of this outpouring of the Spirit, a new factor was released that was shortly to break down the first of the barriers that separated men from their fellows. In the ancient myth of the Tower of Babel (Gen. 11:1 ff.), man's pride and desire to be equal with God had ended in confusion and disharmony, of which difference in language was a symbol. Now, by the coming of the Spirit, Babel was reversed. The power of the Risen Christ, working through his Spirit, now given to the Church, was to begin the process of restoring the harmony that had been broken; reconciling differences among the nations; bridging the gulfs of race, class and speech. By the time Luke wrote this narrative of Pentecost, that had begun to happen. As this festival had commemorated the giving of the Law, which had been the hallmark of the Old Israel, so it marked the real birth of the New Israel, characterized by the presence of the Spirit.

This was now to be the distinctive feature of the New Community. To begin with, it was felt that the clear proof of the presence of the Spirit was its outward expression in ecstatic utterance. The uninhibited emotional atmosphere of a modern Negro revivalist meeting is probably the nearest counterpart to the earliest assemblies of the Church. Beneath that, however, was the inner reality of a new quality of life. It was primarily a sense of liberation, which gradually became more explicit. The New Israel became conscious that it was now free in a deeper sense than its forefathers had been after the first Exodus. From the start they felt that they were freed from their sins, freed from fear of the world and of the future, freed from the power of evil and the supremacy of death. Soon they came to see that they were also freed from the stranglehold of the Law and the damnation that threatened failure to observe its niceties.

This sense of liberation resulted in the characteristic note of joy and buoyancy that pervades the New Testament records. To be in the New Community did mark a man off from his fellows, and it must have been this infectious sense of being on top of the world that drew others into the Christian fellowship as much as anything said by the missionaries—that and the quality of life that the first Christians exhibited in their daily affairs. When St. Paul says that the fruit of the Spirit is love, joy, peace, long-suffering, kindness, goodness, faithfulness, meekness, temperance (Gal. 5:22), he is painting a picture of the kind of life that the best of the earliest Christians in fact practiced. From the first it was clear that the old dichotomy between religious belief and daily behavior had gone forever. For the citizen of the Kingdom, living by the power of the Spirit, Christian belief and Christian practice were two sides of the same coin.

The immediate effect of the experience of Pentecost was to take the gospel into the streets of Jerusalem and launch it on the first stage of its missionary task. Throughout the New Testament we see the enlarging conception of what that meant. Here was a new message and a new power. It must be proclaimed and shared. Despite themselves, their Jewish nationalism and their limited horizons, stage by stage the first missionaries are driven by a power stronger than themselves to spread the gospel in ever-widening circles and in the process reach a deeper understanding of what the gospel really is.

At first the setting and the presentation were wholly Jewish. The apostles themselves and their first converts were men who had been reared in the nursery of Jewish piety. Not only were they schooled in the Scriptures, they were also inheritors of the Law and the Temple. If their compatriots had been asked to say what distinguished the disciples from themselves, they would have answered simply that in every respect except one there was indeed no difference.

These Nazarenes, or followers of the Way, as they were called, frequented the Temple and kept

the Law. It was true that they met together in a
certain Upper Room for prayer meetings, but this
was a harmless practice. Equally harmless was the
one article of belief that their countrymen did not
share, namely that Messiah had come. All good
Jews knew that he would some day appear, but it
was fantastic to allege that the carpenter of
Nazareth who had been crucified only the other
day for blasphemy and imposture could have been
he.

The Nazarenes themselves would have given a
different account of their belief, and some of their
countrymen at any rate were prepared to listen, and
a smaller number still became convinced that these
beliefs were true. The summaries of Peter's two
sermons given by Luke as having been preached
openly after Pentecost are illuminating (Acts 2:3).
They indicate not only the earliest formulation of
Christian doctrine but the nature of the earliest
missionary propaganda and how much both depended on intensive study of the Old Testament.
Peter's claim is that all along the line Scripture was
being fulfilled before their eyes. The day of
YHWH of which the prophets had spoken was
upon them. The signs that Joel had indicated—the
outpouring of God's Spirit and the return of the old
prophetic ecstasy— were already visible. This had
only happened because God had first sent his Messiah. Jesus of Nazareth, of Davidic descent, whose
marvelous acts of power they all remembered, had
been cruelly done to death by his own people.

Yet this had been within God's plan, for Scripture had also said that Messiah must suffer. And

Scripture had further said that God would raise his Messiah from the dead and exalt him to a place of power beside himself. This had now happened, as the Twelve could testify, and this strange new power that had come at Pentecost, which they had all seen with their own eyes, was the result. Jesus, then, had been made Messiah and Lord. Soon he would return to judge the world. To those who repented of their sins, and were baptized into the Kingdom of the Messiah, would be granted forgiveness and the gift of the Holy Spirit. It is clear from these early sermons that at this stage there was no clear-cut theology. The time for precision of thought was not yet. Experience was too overwhelming. The Holy Spirit was "this thing"; Jesus was Messiah, or in the Greek form Christ, the Servant, the Holy One, the Prince of Life, the Savior. In such terms was the gospel first preached. With the mass of the people, it found little acceptance. Those who joined the new fellowship continued outwardly as practicing Jews, with additional meetings for the "breaking of bread," presumably a eucharistic celebration, sharing their possessions as a mark of their common life.

Such a group in the community, if it induced no great support, could rouse little opposition among ordinary folk. The gift of healing that the apostles had inherited from Jesus commended them further. Their boldness was impressive, and their lightheartedness compared favorably with the gloomy prohibitionism of official Jewish religion. The Sadducees first took action against them, on the grounds that any kind of Messianic doctrine was dangerous, as being unacceptable to the Roman overlords, and that in their view any suggestion of resurrection was heretical. The Pharisees, however, under the guidance of Gamaliel, took the attitude that if this new movement was as spurious as other Messianic cults in the past, it would die a natural death. If, however, it was genuine, then the hand of God was in it, and they could not oppose it.

So ends the first period of the Church's history. In calling themselves the Church, as they did at this time, the Nazarenes took over the word *ecclesia*, which they had learned through their reading of the Old Testament to associate with the congregation of Israel. Israel had been God's "chosen people," since that is the essential meaning of ecclesia. In using the same word of themselves, the Nazarenes clearly asserted the historic continuity of the New Israel with the Old. That such continuity did not involve identity was now to become apparent.

II

The World Church

The second phase of the Church's development is marked by the beginning of the process whereby it detached itself from its Jewish setting and became a worldwide movement. Since the days before the Exile, Jewry had, by choice and compulsion, become a migratory folk. As merchants, soldiers, prisoners or fugitives, Jews had established themselves throughout the Mediterranean world. By New Testament times there were many more Jews outside Palestine than inside. However much they kept to themselves, they could not fail to be affected by the Gentile communities in which they lived.

While the Temple of Jerusalem remained their spiritual home, which they supported by a voluntary tax, and although every exiled Jew regarded pilgrimages to Jerusalem as a pious duty, the religious life of the overseas communities was marked by a vitality that was not apparent in the homeland. Judaism abroad had become a missionary religion.

Intelligent pagans were attracted by the austere services of the synagogue, the high ethical tone of the Law and the wholesomeness of Jewish family life. The Empire was deteriorating morally and spiritually. The tone was set by a profligate court, and the institution of slavery had sown dragons' teeth that were being reaped in the corruption of society. The public stage and the arena assisted the lowering of standards and the decline of taste. The marriage bond meant little; organized prostitution and sexual perversion were rife. Pagan religion offered little guidance. The gods were discredited and the priesthood despised. Common folk sought solace in the mystery cults, while the more intelligent turned to the philosophers.

Some, however, found what they sought in the religion of the Jews. Unwilling to comply with all that the Law demanded of converts to Judaism, including circumcision, observance of ceremonial obligations and dietary regulations, pagans who were attracted to the Jewish faith found themselves satisfied to remain as adherents of the synagogues, studying the Scriptures, and worshiping the God whom Israel had taught them to know.

This development had, however, a reciprocal effect. While not abating one whit their devotion to the Law, their racial pride or their conviction that the way to God lay through his Chosen People, contact with the pagan world meant that overseas Jews were saved from the parochialism, the narrow exclusiveness and spiritual stagnation of their compatriots in Jerusalem. They spoke Greek and their Scriptures were Greek, as were their dress, their manners and often their names.

The civilized world was their parish, and something of its liberating influences and universal outlook attached itself to their religious attitude. If any such Jews were to become convinced that Peter and the other apostles were right, a new spirit would inevitably enter the Christian community. This is in fact what happened, and it is due to two such overseas Jews, Stephen and Paul, that Christianity was saved from dying out as a sect of Judaism and became instead a worldwide faith.

The Book of Acts reveals (6:1 ff.) that already, a year or two after the Resurrection, the Church had grown considerably and that there were now two elements in the Christian community. There was the original orthodox conservative line, represented and led by the Twelve, content to regard the New Israel as continuous with the Old and happy to leave it within the framework of the Temple and the Law. The gospel was for the Jews, the heirs of the Covenant and the Promise. Messiah's Kingdom was a Jewish preserve.

Beside that, however, was a new and radical party, consisting of overseas Jews now resident in Jerusalem. These Greek-speaking Jewish Christians, while acknowledging the authority of the Twelve, had secured official rank within the Church for seven of their number, the leader of whom was Stephen, a man of obviously outstanding ability. He lost no time in engaging in disputations with the rabbis and was hauled before the Sanhedrin on a charge of blasphemy.

His defense was to carry the battle into the enemy's camp. In a masterly speech (Acts 7:2 ff.), he attacked the most jealously held convictions of the Jewish faith: that they were divinely appointed

custodians of God's Holy Land, Holy Temple and
Holy Law. Stephen draws on the history they all
know to point out that God revealed himself to
Abraham and Moses before Israel had any stake in
Canaan. In building a Temple, Solomon not only
flouted the intentions of his great father David, but
defied Scripture itself. As for the Law, from the
time of Moses onward, Israel had treated it with
contempt, killed God's prophets who foretold the
coming of Messiah, and now, consistent in its vil-
lainy, had murdered Messiah himself. The Old Israel had failed, and God had created for himself a
New People.

Beside themselves with rage, the Sanhedrin had
Stephen dragged out and stoned to death. The first
Christian martyr, like his Master, died with a prayer
on his lips for his enemies. One of these enemies,
standing by and watching his execution, was Rabbi
Saul of Tarsus. St. Augustine dated the beginning
of Paul's conversion from that moment. "If Stephen had not prayed, the Church would not have
Paul."

This new recalcitrancy among the hitherto com-
plaisant Nazarenes put an end to the tolerance that
had been extended to them by the Pharisaic party.
The conservative section of the Church, meticulous
in the respect it paid to Jewish institutions, was left
in peace, but the wrath of the Sanhedrin fell upon
the radical party, whose support of Stephen marked
them as traitors to their national heritage. The first
persecution, prominent in which was Saul of Tarsus, whose venom and ruthlessness made him a
veritable Torquemada, had the effect of driving

Stephen's sympathizers out of Jerusalem and scattering them throughout Palestine. Not for the first time, however, the blood of the martyrs proved to be the seed of the Church, for wherever they went the infectious power of their faith and their missionary zeal were such that new Christian cells were created up and down the country.

Thus began the expansion of Christianity. There follows a period in which the power of God contained in the gospel forces the Church despite itself into the wider world. We get the impression on the one hand of cautious, conservative Church leaders at Jerusalem, anxious to make the best of both worlds, Jewish and Christian, apparently still sufficiently orthodox to be personae gratae with the rabbis, and on the other hand of the real work of the Church being done by pioneers like Philip, who became apostle to the once-hated Samaritans. His encounter with a God-fearing pagan, who was subsequently baptized into the Christian Ecclesia, marks a further stage in the barrier-breaking power of the gospel (Acts 8:26 ff.).

Peter himself became convinced that it was the will of God that Gentiles should also be eligible for the Messianic community, and an important precedent was set when he baptized a Roman legionary (Acts 10:1 ff.). While this official action was taken, the unofficial mission went on apace, principally to the Jews as far afield as Cyprus, but at Antioch in Syria, for the first time a direct approach was made to the Gentiles. The result surpassed expectations. Large numbers of pagans turned to the new faith, and Antioch became the first center of a non-Jewish

Church. It was here that the Nazarenes were for the first time called Christians.

Meantime it appears that the Twelve were no longer in supreme authority. Death and persecution had broken their ranks. The mother Church was still Jerusalem, but its leadership had passed into the hands of the ultraconservative and pro-Jewish James, who was probably the author of the New Testament letter of that name, and it was to become progressively more and more a symbol and a figurehead. The real driving force of Christianity was to be found in the Gentile Christian community at Antioch, led now, by an extraordinary turn of history, by that recent scourge of the saints, Paul of Tarsus.

An overseas Jew from the great Greek city of Tarsus in Asia Minor, Saul had been brought up in the strictest Jewish mental disciplines by his Pharisaic father and had studied in his early days under Gamaliel in Jerusalem, to which he had returned as a rabbi shortly after the Resurrection. His first contact with the new faith seems to have been made when Stephen and his associates had drawn the unfavorable attention of the Jewish authorities by their outrageous attack on the established religion. Paul and Stephen were well matched. Both were extremely able men. Paul was at once aware, unlike many of his coreligionists, that this new heresy was not a passing phase but was a movement that threatened the very fabric of the Law and the State and the distinctive role that God had given to Israel.

Accordingly it was his business by argument and

force to suppress it. In the persecution that followed Stephen's murder, Paul's vindictiveness knew no bounds. He would root out this pestilence and affront to God—harrying, imprisoning, killing men and women who in his eyes were guilty of blasphemy, treason and sacrilege. It was while this passionate and cruel man was on his way to Damascus, armed with authority to arrest any followers of the new heresy he could find there, that the incredible happened.

No one but Paul himself can say what took place. His own testimony is that instead of arresting Christians, he himself was arrested by Christ (Phil. 3: 12). In the evidence he gives in his letters and speeches, the consistent element is that the Risen Christ appeared to him as he had appeared to the disciples (1 Cor. 15:8; Acts 9, 22, 26). Paul saw him no longer as the seducer of the faithful but as God's Messiah. From that moment he became a man in Christ, devoting all his prodigious energy, skill and courage, and the resources of a remarkable mind, to the advancing of the cause he had set out to destroy.

It may well be that, as Augustine suggested, this conversion experience marked the culmination of a long process of growing doubt in Paul's mind. He must have been struck by the behavior of such men as Stephen compared with his own, by the evidence of the Scriptures, by the hopelessness of fulfilling the precepts of the Law, and by the consequent sense of frustration within himself (Rom. 7). His inward misgivings would account for the ferocity of his actions. Be that as it may, there is perhaps no event which is so significant for Western civilization as the conversion of Paul. From this date, probably A.D. 33, until his death, which tradition gives as A.D. 64, during the first Roman persecution of the Christians under Nero, he lived for his faith and his Master. St. Luke's vivid narrative depicts in brilliant pen pictures the magnitude of Paul's task and the courage and tenacity with which it was accomplished.

After several years of mental readjustment and experimental evangelism, mostly in his own part of the world, Paul found himself summoned to the leadership of the most vital center of Christianity, Antioch. From this base, Paul conducted in ever-widening circles a work of missionary enterprise that brought the Christian faith eventually to the capital of the Empire. Christian communities were founded by him or his followers throughout the Mediterranean world. By constant visitation and by writing letters, he consolidated the work, answered questions, solved problems, gave encouragement, administered rebukes. There is no attempt to disguise the opposition or the failures or to gloss over the shortcomings of the missionaries themselves.

Threatened, beaten, imprisoned, slandered, misunderstood and thwarted, Paul gives no indication that he ever weakened either in faith or resolution. Against a solid mass of indifference, superstition and vice among the pagans, and violent and abusive attacks from his Jewish countrymen, Paul and his handful of fellow workers laid the foundations of the World Church. He had not only to contend with violence from his enemies, but he had to also placate the timid leaders of the Jerusalem Church, who were with difficulty persuaded that Christianity must be a universal faith if it was to be true to its Founder.

One by one the barriers went down, as Jews, Samaritans and Gentiles, men and women, slaves and freedmen, found themselves side by side in a new kind of community, sharing a new hope, a new quality of life, and bound by a common loyalty. To the simple pagans, Christianity offered what they had sought in the mystery cults: liberation from fear and death. To the more thoughtful among them, it fulfilled what the best of their philosophy had taught about the purpose of life, and to those who had already been attracted by Judaism, it offered the essence of Israel's legacy without the restrictions of Jewish nationalism or Jewish Law.

With this universalism inherent in itself, Christianity made its way into the very heart of the pagan world. It was furthered in its advance by the existence of the Pax Romana, which ensured unhindered progress to the missionaries, and by the great Imperial roads, along which the gospel rapidly spread. There was, too, at this point in history the fact of a common language, colloquial Greek, understood and spoken as a second tongue by all except barbarians, which meant that the proclamation of the gospel could reach the furthest confines of the Empire.

In the story of its advance, we are not taken by the Bible further than the end of the work of Paul. And it is enough. The foundations had been laid. The Church had shown that although it carried in it the heritage of Israel, its message was to the whole world. From the capital of the Empire where the history of the Book of Acts leaves off, the Church proceeded to the fulfillment of its appointed mission.

III

Reinterpretation

Thus there is the astonishing fact to be reckoned with that a faith that began in a wholly Jewish setting, based on Jewish theology, founded by a Jew and propagated by Jews, most of whom had great difficulty in bringing themselves to admit that it could ever be the will of God that the new faith should embrace any others than Jews, had in thirty years attracted to itself a vast preponderance of men and women of diverse background, faith and culture, to most of whom Jerusalem and the Jews had been little more than a name.

It is not enough to say that this was due to the accidents of history: a common language, easy communications and a world at peace. Nor does it explain the transition to point to the Jewish synagogues throughout the cities of the Empire, where, already, Gentiles who were dissatisfied with what was offered to them by their own religious and ethical systems had learned to find in these Jewish oases the answer to the deeper questions that perplexed them.

Doubtless these factors played a part, and a large part. Christian missionaries were quick to seize on the pagan fringe of the synagogues as the most profitable point of contact with the Gentile world. They also had powerful assistance from the fact that at that time the confusion of religious and moral ideas through the crosscurrents of Oriental and Western thought was so great that any clear or convincing advocacy of a new faith stood a large chance of success.

It would be nearer the mark to attribute the success of Christianity in the pagan world to the genius of Paul. Without doubt he was the mastermind that grasped the magnitude of the task and saw most deeply into the thought and intention of Jesus. It was Paul who perceived that even if it meant a battle with the conservative Jerusalem leadership, he must fight for the rights of Gentile converts to come into the Church on their own rights and not to be tied to the pettifogging regulations that meant so much to the Jewish section.

Thus by securing for his pagan converts freedom from the necessity of circumcision and abstention from forbidden food, which seemed to the conservatives to be the will of God for the new faith, as it had been for the old, Paul unquestionably increased the appeal of Christianity for the vast majority of pagans, who otherwise would have left it severely alone or remained adherents on its fringe.

By his victory at the Council of Jerusalem, the first assembly of the Church, in A.D. 49, Paul established this principle. Henceforth, whatever distinctive Jewish practices continued to be of the essence of Christianity for those who had been brought up under the Old Testament dispensation, for those who came from other traditions, no such obligation would be insisted on. Yet while the principle was agreed to, the measure of Paul's tenacity of purpose is to be seen in the constant struggle in which he had to engage to ensure that the agreement was honored. Time and again the life of some Gentile community or other was threatened with disruption because the Jewish section of the Church tried to insist on the provisions of the Law being accepted by all Christians.

It would be misleading, however, to focus attention upon Paul as if he were the sole architect of the Church as we know it, and Paul himself would have been the first to say so. The truth is rather that the development of Christianity, from being to all appearances a Jewish sect into a universal faith, took place as and when Christians perceived more clearly what had been the place in history of Jesus himself and what had been the scope of his purpose. It was the dynamic of the gospel itself, and the Spirit of Christ active within the Church, which made this development inevitable.

When we read the Synoptic gospels, we are left with the impression of a predominantly Jewish milieu. Thought forms and terminology as well as locality are Palestinian. When we turn to the rest of the New Testament, the milieu is Imperial. We are in a Gentile world. Problems are different, answers are different. We are no longer in a world where Messiah, Kingdom of God, the Servant, the Son of Man, are the current expressions. We find instead such phrases as Eternal Life, Son of God, Body of Christ. Nothing could be further from the truth than to conclude that the Church that emerged in the Roman Empire was different in character and belief from that of the early days in Jerusalem.

What had happened was simply this: that just as the gospel was the fulfillment of the Law and the prophets, so the World Church was the fulfillment of the gospel. Jesus did not reject the Old Testament or supersede it. What he rejected was the travesty of the Law and the prophets that Judaism had become. It was the elaboration of ceremonial, the paraphernalia of the Temple, the deadweight of moral obligations, the spiritual arrogance, the racial exclusiveness, all of which Jerusalem encouraged, as being the proper witness of the People of God, that drew forth Jesus' wrath and incurred his sternest condemnation.

The God whom Jesus knew and loved was the God of Jeremiah, Amos, Hosea, Isaiah and Micah. The morality that Jesus commended was the essence of the Mosaic Law. The community that he founded was continuous with Abraham and the fathers, with Elijah and the seven thousand who did not bow the knee to Baal. It was new, but it was a new Israel. It was the reconstituted People of God, reformed and cleansed, and given again its proper direction.

Similarly, the form in which the New Israel was first proclaimed was of necessity essentially Jewish. It was being preached to Jews to whom the terms Messiah, Kingdom, David meant everything. From allusions in Paul's letters (Rom. 1:2-5; 1 Thess. 1:9-10), we gather that it was in this ultra-Jewish form that he himself as a missionary, after his conversion, was introduced to the gospel and at first proclaimed it. This was the common form of the preaching for a Jewish audience.

Paul was converted in A.D. 33. His first letter was, however, not written until A.D. 49 at the earliest. In these intervening years, what had taken place in Paul's mind was a rethinking of his Old Testament faith in the new light of his conversion experience. But, as he realized, this had now to be proclaimed to men and women who knew little or nothing of the Jews and their Scriptures. Accordingly he had to strike a balance between being faithful to the historic significance of Israel as the People of God, the people to whom God had chosen to reveal himself, and presenting this in a way that would mean something to pagan minds. The essence of the divine revelation to Israel, and the unique significance of Jesus, must be preserved, but they must be restated in the language of the wider world.

In so doing Paul was grappling with a problem that faced the other New Testament writers as well. All that is contained in the New Testament, in its present finished form, with the exception of Paul's letters, was written after the historical period covered by the Book of Acts had ended. It was indeed the persecution of the Christians in Rome in A.D. 64, in response to Nero's demand to find a scapegoat for the great fire that destroyed much of the city, which gave the impetus to the writing of the gospels.

Mark, Matthew and Luke, since they are mainly concerned with giving a record of the events of

Jesus' ministry, his Life, Death and Resurrection, are necessarily Palestinian in their atmosphere. But when we turn to the other writings of the New Testament, which were for the most part directed toward non-Jewish readers, we observe, as in the case of Paul, this same twin purpose: to preserve the historic continuity with Israel and at the same time to speak in language that non-Jews would understand.

None of these writers was a systematic theologian, least of all Paul himself. The day of precise definition, of creed making, of attempting to state in clear-cut doctrinal terms to the world at large what Christianity was, lay well ahead and is outside the biblical period. The beginning of the process, however, can be seen in the New Testament documents. Its beginning, as its completion in the creeds, was necessary in order to make plain what Christianity was not, as much as what it was, and to present a reasonable faith to enquiring minds.

We may take as illustrative of this process within the New Testament period three types of approach: that of the letter to the Hebrews, the letters of Paul and the gospel of John. As we should expect, the letter to the Hebrews, being written to conservative Jewish Christians, probably in Rome, by an unknown Christian author living in Alexandria, betrays most strongly the Jewish background of the Christian faith. The writer, addressing readers to whom the Temple, its priesthood and its sacrifices had meant much, uses this as the point of departure for his message.

The recipients of the letter were apparently inclined to confuse Christianity with Judaism. Accordingly the writer, often using obscure Old Testament allusions that could have meaning only for Jews, makes his point that to exchange Christianity for Judaism is to barter substance for shadow. Incorporating, significantly, Plato's concept of the heavenly ideal and the earthly reflection, he describes the practices of Judaism and the faith of the Old Testament as the imperfect earthly reflection of the perfect heavenly reality of Christ himself. The priesthood, the Temple, its altars and its sacrifices, were the earthly counterparts of the heavenly reality. Priests, altar, sacrifices were fallible, earthbound attempts to bridge the gulf between God and man. Only the ideal High Priest, who offered himself once for all as the perfect sacrifice, could make the sinner at one with God.

To Jews, schooled in the sacrificial system and doubtless nostalgically conscious of the appeal of tradition, such an approach could not fail to be impressive. Yet when the writer to the Hebrews used this argument, he was not writing as a Jew but as a Christian, as one who remembered that Jesus himself had spoken of his Death as the self-giving of the Servant, a ransom for many (Mark 10:45), and who remembered that one of the basic elements in the earliest preaching was that Christ died for our sins, according to the Scriptures (1 Cor. 15:3).

Paul stands midway between the writer of Hebrews and the author of the fourth gospel. Himself a Jew, yet conscious of being the apostle to the Gentiles, writing to communities that had in them

both Jewish and Gentile converts, he blends Old
Testament thought and Jewish background with an
approach that would, at the same time, be meaning-
ful to the pagan world.

Thus in the great passage in his letter to the
Ephesians (2:11-22), where he is addressing a
predominantly non-Jewish community, his emphasis is on the fact that through Christ a new type of
man has come into existence, the Christian man,
who is neither Jew nor Gentile. Through faith in
Christ, Jews and Gentiles, at peace with one another, become part of the family of God the Father
and share together the religious heritage of Israel.
Yet here again Paul does no more than make explicit Jesus' parable of the multitude of outcasts in
Jewish eyes, gathered from the highways and by-
ways, who would share the banquet of the Messianic Kingdom (Matt. 22:1-13).

The fourth gospel goes furthest in the New Testament toward restating the significance of Jesus
and the essence of the gospel in terms of current
thought. Written toward the end of the first century
in the pagan atmosphere of Asia Minor, this gospel
has raised many questions, not least because of its
difference in tone from that of the other three. Yet
this is surely its greatest merit: it seeks to retain
contact with the historical Jesus while expressing in
words that conveyed most meaning to its readers
the deepest truth of a gospel that is beyond place
and time.

Jesus is presented to the pagan world as the Way,
the Truth and the Life. He is the Bread of Life, the
Light of the World, the Good Shepherd and the

Vine. Messiah is translated as Son of God; the "Kingdom" becomes "Eternal Life." The culmination of the attempt of this writer to assert in his own day and place the unchanging relevance of the gospel is to be seen in his claim that the Word became flesh (1:14). To the Greek mind the Word meant the Logos, the creative purpose behind the universe. To the Hebrew mind it recalled the first chapter of the Book of Genesis and the Word that made heaven and earth. It also meant the Wisdom of God and the Word that he spoke through the prophets. The fourth gospel, therefore, is presenting Jesus to the pagan world not as the Prophet of Nazareth, nor the Jewish Messiah, but as the full expression in human terms of the mind and purpose of God.

The Bible in the Twentieth Century

This work of reinterpreting and restating the essential elements in the biblical record, which had already begun in New Testament times, indicates the line that must be followed in presenting the Bible in the twentieth century. Neither Paul nor the author of the fourth gospel regarded the thought forms and terminology of Old Testament or gospels as sacrosanct or endowed with mystical significance, but attempted, while retaining a firm grasp of the historical background and the substance of the revelation, to translate them into language and processes of thought that were more familiar to their readers.

If we are to follow their example in teaching and preaching to minds to which Palestine and the Jewish setting of the Bible seem remote and unreal, we must attempt somehow to steer a middle course between a fruitless effort to reinstate biblical words and ideas that are now merely lifeless relics of the past, and the equally profitless and more dangerous endeavor to lose contact with the historical basis and restate the Bible in the terminology of Marx or Freud or the Existentialists.

Nor is there anything to be gained by the cry of: Back to Aquinas! or Back to the Reformers! If we believe at all in the power of the Spirit to illumine the minds of each age and guide them into an understanding of what God is saying to us through the Scriptures, we cannot allow that he has less to say to us today than to past ages, or that he cannot say it in the language of our time.

Accordingly, while not abating one whit its primary obligation of ascertaining by careful scholarship, linguistic study and critical research the original text and meaning of the biblical documents, the Church's next duty is to see to it that by using up-to-date translations, by readily availing itself of all the new light that the various branches of science can supply, our twentieth-century people can recognize at once that there in the Bible is a message that is timeless, as relevant today as when it was first written.

The theme of the Bible is the story of God's plan to recreate the world. The divine intention, outlined in Genesis 1, that men should fully reflect the image of God in which they are made, is thwarted by the selfishness and devilry of mankind in the mass. Yet it is not God's will that man should destroy himself by his own folly but that he should be won back to the true relationship to God and find his proper place in the universe.

Since the true obedience of God is woven into the texture of daily life and finds expression in the attitudes and actions of men in society, it is necessary that the road back to God should be indicated on the plane of history. Accordingly God chooses a living community to be the means of bringing the world and all its peoples to the knowledge of the nature of reality and of how they may live in harmony with that reality and with one another.

Men must be taught by bitter experience, by trial and error, the lessons of life. They have to learn the hard way that they must lose themselves to find themselves and that self-giving is the path to self-fulfillment. They must know not only that tolerance, charity and justice are incumbent upon them as means to the well-being of all, but that these lead to such well-being precisely because they are reflections of the nature of Reality itself.

Such lessons cannot be learned by instinct. Left to ourselves and our own inclinations, we sink to the level of the jungle. Without guidance and help from beyond himself, man's best efforts and intentions end in disaster.

The message of the Bible is that such help and guidance is given. We are shown how a tiny and otherwise unimportant nation was granted an insight into the meaning of life and the nature of the universe. There was communicated to Israel, through the minds of a series of devout and sensitive men, an understanding of history and the power that molds it that was unique in human experience. Despite their proclamation of what they saw to be the true nature of things, and their attempts to bring the life of their society into harmony with the purpose of God for men, they were unable to induce their nation to fulfill what they conceived to be its appointed role. Israel, as they saw, had been singled out to exhibit in its national life the qualities of integrity and mercy, mutual service and personal piety, which should convince the world that this was the divine pattern for all societies.

Instead of that, Israel succumbed to sensuality, luxury and avarice; distorted the worship of God; perverted the rights of men and ended the first phase of their history in catastrophe. Given a fresh start, and without the temptations of power and prestige, they fell victims to spiritual arrogance, religious pride and hypocrisy, and were rejected as no longer useful channels of the divine revelation.

Yet the light of that revelation had never been wholly extinguished. Within the nation, the true People of God had maintained their minority witness throughout the centuries. The line of Abraham, Moses and the prophets, and those who shared their high sense of vocation, ensured that Israel never wholly betrayed its mission. It was through them that the lessons that were learned, as well as the warnings that went unheeded, were handed on in the pages of Scripture, interwoven with the lives of the men and women who made up the nation's story, and who are of significance to posterity as having either responded to God's call or failed to do so.

It is because of this minority witness, the consecrated group within the nation, which persisted down the centuries, that we cannot write off Israel's history as one of total failure. It is because of them that the Old Testament takes its place beside the New, not as the record of a lost cause but as the preparation for a greater revelation.

Taken together, Old and New Testaments con-

stitute a single story, that of the creation and development of a People of God, a divine common-
wealth. Beginning within the national community
of Israel, and reborn as the supranational community of the New Israel, the Christian Church finds
in the Bible its title deeds, the record of its growth
and the scope of its purpose. It is God's instrument
called to fulfill the task in which Israel failed, and
enabled to perform it by a power that was not given
to Israel, that of the Son of God himself.

St. Teresa said that Christ had no other hands or
feet in the world but those of the members of his
Church. God's recreation of mankind and the
renewal of its life, effected in principle through
Christ, can only be carried out by his servants. The
Church is, therefore, in the world committed to the
task of renewing society in all its aspects. It is to
present in itself an example of the perfect obedience of God, the life that the People of God should
live in the world, as disciples of him who said,
"You must be perfect as your Heavenly Father is
perfect" (Matt. 5:48). By its work and witness, the
Church is committed to the task of bringing the
whole political, social and economic order, together with the personal life of all his people, under
the power and influence of Christ.

"God was in Christ reconciling the world to
Himself" (2 Cor. 5:19). By the forgiveness of sins,
the healing of men's minds and bodies, and by his
conquest of death, Christ gave a token and a pledge
not only of God's will but of God's power to do this
for all. In principle the battle has been won.
Through Christ, God has revealed his purpose that

all mankind should be gathered into his family as sons and daughters of a heavenly Father. By his Life, Death and Resurrection, Christ has bridged the gulf between God and man and made us at one with him. To those who commit themselves to God and pledge themselves to his service in the fellowship of the Church, there is offered the high privilege of cooperating with God in this work of reconciliation. It is God's will that men should live in peace and charity; that barriers between man and man should be broken down; that truth and justice, courtesy and integrity, compassion and kindness should be the marks of private and public life.

The Church is called to the task of proclaiming the need for God-centered lives and a God-centered world. But the task, like that of her Master, is not merely one of proclamation but of action, in healing divisions, restoring life, making men whole in mind and body. Thus the permeation of medicine, education, politics and economics, by men and women committed to Christ, is the paramount need of the world and the first call upon the loyalty of Churchmen.

The Bible presents us with the spectacle of societies that attempted to manage their affairs in defiance of God, and of one society in particular which, though officially committed to his service, exhibited most of the vices and follies of its neighbors. The biblical warning is that the disasters that befell them fall in like manner on all societies that similarly ignore or travesty the laws on which the universe is founded.

The Bible also, however, demonstrates the

power of the few to influence the many and shows that we are not puppets in a prearranged performance, but that men and women who are in the right relationship to God can by his power change the course of history.

Thus the biblical view of life and the world is in the first place pessimistic. It sees the failure and stupidity of men as the normal texture of life. Greed and malice, self-interest and concupiscence, hate and cruelty, are so ingrained in man's nature that, humanly speaking, there is little reason to expect anything but that history should show a recurring pattern of war and strife, bitterness and confusion, pain and fear.

Yet the biblical insights teach us that this pattern is not God's will for the world and that he has provided the means to change it. Through the power of Christ, a new factor has been released, working through those who are pledged to his service and are part of his body, the Church. Perfect love to God and to one's neighbors is something that has never been fully exhibited in this world except in Christ himself. Yet when it has been most closely approximated in the lives of Christian men and women in all ages, the effect on the life of society has given an earnest of its power to heal wounds, banish fear, assuage pain and conquer hatred. Instead of deploring the failure of the Church, we should marvel that in the brief moment of man's existence on this planet represented by the last two thousand years of history, so much has indeed been achieved. The power of the gospel to change human nature, and the complex organism that we call the world, has been evidenced in every page of mankind's story for twenty centuries.

To play a part in this redemptive work is the endeavor to which the Bible summons each one of us. It does not promise an easier path than that which lay before prophets and saints. It does not minimize the power of evil or the intractable elements in human nature. There is no illusion in the minds of the biblical writers about an eventual Paradise on earth. The picture is rather one of conflict between good and evil until the end of time.

But the Bible sees every man who has taken his stand on the side of God as already a citizen of two worlds: this imperfect world in which we live and the perfect realm of God. To be committed to Christ is to be anchored to One who is supreme over the hazards of fortune and stronger than death itself. The life of the Christian is hid with Christ in God, and that life is something that begins here and now and is deepened and enriched in the mystery that lies beyond.

The biblical writers could, no more than we ourselves, talk of what lies beyond the human experience of each of us or what awaits us on the other side of time and history, except in the language of symbolism and poetry. But as the Book of Genesis begins with the claim that man is created to be a child of God, so the Book of Revelation ends with the assertion that the consummation of all things is that this purpose of God will be accomplished.

To the first generation of Christians, it seemed that the world beyond lay on their doorstep. So strong was their sense of living in the presence of the supernatural, that the end of the present world and the triumph of Christ seemed at any moment about to take place. With the passing of the years, they learned that the formidable task to which the Church had been called was not one of decades but of millennia. Yet their conviction never wavered that however long it might take, the ultimate victory of good and destruction of evil was a certainty. The decisive battle had been won. D-Day had come, and V-Day was therefore assured.

Besides the pessimism with which it regards man as he is, the Bible, therefore, is optimistic about man and the world as they will be. What it says about the future is not pious hope or speculation but conviction based on what has already happened. It sees the coming of Christ as the beginning of the end, and the world as now living in expectation of a final victory. For the twentieth-century Christian, as for the first-century Christian, that means that life here and now is a call to don the whole armor of God (Eph. 6:11) and do battle in the name of Christ against the evil in ourselves and in society, confident that "we are more than conquerors through him who loved us" and that "Neither death nor life . . . nor anything else in all creation will be able to part us from God's love in Christ Jesus our Lord" (Rom. 8:37–39).